Judo
through the
Looking Glass

Jerry Hicks

"Where echoes live in memory yet
Though envious years would say forget."
Lewis Carroll

First published in 1994
by Redcliffe Press Ltd.,
22 Canynge Square, Bristol

© Jerry Hicks

ISBN 1 872971 83 0

British Library Cataloguing in Publication Data
A catalogue record for this book is available from
the British Library

All rights reserved. No part of this publication may be
reproduced, stored in a retrieval system, or transmitted in
any form or by any means, electronic, mechanical,
photocopying, recording or otherwise, without the prior
permission of the publishers.

Typeset by Mayhew Typesetting, Rhayader, Powys
Printed in Great Britain by The Longdunn Press, Bristol

Contents

Introduction	5
The Art of Ju-Jitsu	9
The Race for Supremacy	17
The Moment of Truth	25
The Budokwai	33
The Coveted Black Belt	41
The Wooden Horse	49
Feline Privilege	57
Special Powers	63
The Spanner	71
Davids and Goliaths	79
The Caucus Race	85
The Man who Bit the Belt	93
Cultural Collisions	99
Drake's Drum to the Sound of One Hand Clapping	107
A Bunch of Five	113
The Trial	123
Epilogue	130
Bibliography	133

To the Tribe

Introduction

"You are old, Father William," the young man said,
"And your hair has become very white;
And yet you incessantly stand on your head –
Do you think, at your age, it is right?"

During my adolescence I came, almost by chance, on a book which described in detail the little known cult of "judo". It was, in fact, given to me by my sister in the erroneous belief that it would have a gentle, tranquillising influence on my boisterous disposition.

In those days it was still customary for young men to participate eagerly in vigorous sports, and I unhesitatingly selected judo. The book recommended two clubs, one in London and the other in Tokyo. Due to the prevalent war time circumstances both were inaccessible. Furthermore, my boarding school was evacuated to America and I was the only pupil remaining in a large isolated country house.

Yet, despite the lack of facilities, instructor and fellow participants, it did not occur to me that I might select an activity with wider opportunities. I persevered, at first single handed; then at my new school; later at London University and the city of Bristol; and finally, as a fervent pioneer, throughout the west country and the schools of Britain. The extraordinary events and personalities which my journey embraced, and not least my own absurdities, still strike me as bizarre. They exist most vividly for me as a series of anecdotes; and I make no apologies for that. It's about time someone raised a voice in defence of anecdotes. They've come in for much dismissive condescension recently.

"I'm afraid, Mr Hicks, that all you've had to say during the last twenty years about the decline of school sport, the loss of urban playing fields and tendentious connections between these assertions and an increase in heart disease and juvenile crime is nothing more than a tirade of anecdotal evidence."

Such is the pseudo scientific prejudice I have encountered; but anecdotes have stood the test of time a good deal better than statistics and opinion polls.

Which of us in the civilised world would recall the historic achievements of scientists, painters, warriors and writers but for anecdotes about a falling apple, a perfect circle, a foreign eccentric running starkers hither and thither shouting "Eureka", an interrupted game of bowls and a melancholic Scandinavian's encounter with a grave digger? Indeed much of the Bard's vulgar popularity sprang from his ingenious flair for inventing and dramatising anecdotes – now called "sit com".

However my own cautionary anecdotes owe less to imagination than to a vivid memory for inconsequential detail and dialogue which I discovered in jury service is the essential requirement of our legal system.

"Will you tell the jury in your own words what happened on the night in question. You met a man in a 'pub'! What was the name of the man and the title of the public house? You went with this man, whose name you are conveniently unable to remember, into an alley behind the anonymous public house. . . For what purpose? Will you repeat your answer more loudly for the benefit of the juror afflicted with a hearing impediment. You went into the alley in order to go to the toilet!" (My deafness is a constant source of embarrassment to others.)

Scientific expertise, psychological analysis and statistical conclusions are viewed in our courts of law with justifiable suspicion. But that which the common sense of the jury recognises as reliable, and upon which British Justice very properly depends, is the accumulation of anecdotal trivia. I rest my case.

As with Lewis Carroll, whose memorable stories prompted the title of this collection and the chapters' introductory quotations, most of my yarns were spun for children – our own and those of our closest friends. Summer holidays and Boxing Day gatherings over many years have been occasions for making our own entertainment; and they have probably been the spawning ground of our youngsters' professional talents in the performing arts.

In view of my extensive involvement with judo it is not surprising that Dad's contributions were narratives derived mainly from this esoteric domain. But don't despair! I'm not about to reveal secrets of how to do it or impose a tedious litany of sporting statistics. Interest lies in the underground curiosities to be found down the rabbit hole or through the looking glass. My dedication to the ill defined mayhem called "sport" is curious enough; and my obsession with the paradoxes of an alien culture transplanted into British sport is "Curioser and curioser". But most curious of all are the startling displays of individual eccentricity that erupt from the prosaic confines of schools, committee rooms, stately homes and changing rooms. They transcend their habitat. I sometimes avoid names for reasons of discretion, but I hope this will not obscure the shrewd north country observation, "There's nowt so queer as folk".

Children relish the curious, and were always a delightful audience; but what came as a surprise was the adult enthusiasm for my idiosyncratic adventures – recounted part in private and later on Radio 4. So I've made an attempt to bring chronological order to this ramshackle collection which was not written in sequence. If their presentation in book form results in repetition, and if Japanese terminology is confusing your bewilderment will not be inappropriate.

The Art of Ju-Jitsu

In another minute Alice was through the glass and had jumped down into Looking-glass room.

The cellar was dimly lit. I stood in front of the looking-glass with the book in one hand. It was a small green paper back entitled *The Art of Ju-Jitsu*. Instructions in Chapter 3 sounded authentic and were very explicit.

"In the opinion of experts the most effective attitude to assume whilst awaiting an opponent's attack before closing is to stand with head erect, arms held loosely at the sides, feet separated and knees unbent. It is styled in Japanese 'shizenhontai'."

I lowered the book and checked my "shizenhontai". It looked quite impressive; but this was the easy part of my nightly ritual. "Tricks of Throwing" and "Tricks of Groundwork" were far more difficult. At thirteen years old I did not feel the intricacies were beyond me, but I was desperately ill equipped. I had no authentic clothing to wear, no mats on which to fall and, most disturbing of all, I had no partner with whom to practise. There was only one other person in our vast domain and she was over eighty.

My curious isolation in the cellars of a Neo-Georgian country mansion was a freak of war time emergency. It was the autumn of 1940 and a few months previously the building had resounded with the hullabaloo of the Actors' Orphanage. However during the summer Noel Coward and Gertrude Lawrence had arranged the evacuation of the entire school to Hollywood. I had been the only child to decline.

The temptation to seek temporary adoption by Errol Flynn, Gary Cooper or Douglas Fairbanks Junior had been immense. They were the heroes of our wildest fantasies and inspired hazardous feats of daring on the roofs of the Orphanage and up the tallest trees of Mr Tulk's private wood. The prospect of sharing a home with Robin Hood was overwhelming. Nevertheless my father's untimely death, which had procured entry into the delightfully eccentric life of the Orphanage, had also left me as male head of the family. I could not leave my mother and sister to face the Hun unprotected.

Government leaflets left us in little doubt that Hitler's army could arrive any day. We were invited to misdirect strangers who would probably be enemy parachutists in disguise, to remember that "Careless Talk Costs Lives" and, when the enemy jackboot finally came stomping through our towns and villages, to "STAY PUT". Panic stricken civilians on the roads would impede the home army.

Identity cards and gas masks were carried at all times, improvised road blocks were constructed, windows were criss-crossed with sticky brown paper to reduce flying glass and we all were repeatedly warned that showing a light during the blackout was a serious offence. Indeed real life adventure in Britain almost matched the thrills of Saturday morning serials at the cinema.

After an exciting summer holiday when incendiary bombs fell in the next street and an enemy plane flew low enough in daylight for me to see the pilot I returned in a turbulent state of mind to a school without staff or fellow pupils. The secretary and her elderly mother were maintaining sole occupation. I was given brusque instructions:

"We haven't decided what to do with you yet Jerry. Sleep in the cellar for safety, and keep out of mischief. There's a war on you know, so you must pull your weight. Help mother with washing up, laying the table and that sort of thing. We can't squander money on coal so gather plenty of firewood from the grounds. And whatever you do don't forget to do the blackout . . ." There was no mention of education.

I was unexpectedly troubled by this omission. My father had impressed on me the value of a "liberal education" and had introduced me to free libraries. The purposeful resolve with which Sherlock Holmes had educated himself in preparation for his unique career was a worthy example. Yet here was I, desperately ignorant of how to combat an imminent invasion, being advised to wash up and keep out of mischief. Women sometimes took a very tiresome and trivial view of life's great adventures.

The school library was full of books devoid of any information on improvising defence against a modern army. In a radio speech Churchill had said we would never surrender, and I fully supported him. He was keen to fight on the beaches, in the valleys and in the hills. This seemed rather ambitious. I preferred our chances as a guerrilla army restricted to the hills. Perhaps he was speaking figuratively. He often did.

Unfortunately there was an acute shortage of weapons. It had not escaped my attention that the Civil Defence were training with wooden rifles. No wonder we were told to STAY PUT. Our chances of resisting Hitler's might with symbolic weapons in a figurative terrain seemed slight. I therefore deemed it imperative to place at the top of my secret education curriculum alternative forms of combat.

The only serviceable weapon I possessed was a Scout's hand axe; so during extended searches for firewood I practised throwing it at trees. It was difficult to make it stick in; and, although I reassured myself that whichever way it struck a fifth columnist from behind there was at least a chance of disablement, I had misgivings about its wider efficiency.

Peter Fleming's book *Brazilian Adventure* prompted the conversion of a piece of abandoned copper tubing into a blowpipe. I made darts from needles bound with horse hair, and could soon score hits within the chalked outline of a human figure from seven paces. Unluckily none of the local chemists stocked the deadly native poison curare. Without it pricks from my darts, however painful, might do little more than provoke brutal retaliation.

I persevered with making a spear, a bow and arrow and a bolas; but outdoor trials convinced me that none was a match for the German Luger. Within a month I was forced to conclude that the most practical option of last resort was skilful unarmed combat.

It was at this critical period of decision that *The Art of Ju-Jitsu* fell into my hands. All at once a source of power which hitherto had seemed tantalisingly elusive was within reach. My library reading had divulged numerous hints of oriental fighting skills which bordered on the occult. Sherlock Holmes' miraculous escape from the fiendish clutches of Moriarty at the Reichenbach Falls was achieved by the great detective's mastery of Bartitsu; Bulldog Drummond struck terror into the German Army during the First World War with a deadly neck lock taught to him in secret by a wily Japanese; and perhaps the most unexpected hero of the cinema was the enigmatic Mr Moto (alias Peter Lorre) who could dispatch half a dozen thugs, each twice his size, by the bewildering application of ju-jitsu.

There could be little doubt that the techniques used by these fictional heroes had a genuine basis in fact. Indeed I had read of a diminutive Japanese wrestler called Yukio Tani who had challenged in vain the legendary strong men of the music halls – Hackenschmidt and Sandow. Neither would risk his reputation since none of Tani's opponents had survived the requisite three minutes to claim the £5 on offer. Perhaps with his knowledge even a thirteen year old school boy could overcome a German fifth columnist.

"Professor Yukio Tani is a name to conjure with," said the author of my little green book; and conjure I did. Since his name appeared on the cover, I had mistakenly assumed that this real life legend was himself the author, and suffered brief disappointment when I discovered that the mysteries of the Orient were being disclosed by a Mr E.J. Harrison. However I was quickly cheered to read that the writer was a 3rd Dan holder of "the coveted black belt", and that he had earned this distinction in Japan. He also knew Professor Tani who commended him in the foreword. I re-read the cover. It said:

> written under the auspices of
> PROFESSOR YUKIO TANI

and a new word was added to my vocabulary.

Thus reassured I turned immediately to the practical instruction which commenced in Chapter 3. Historical introductions would have to wait.

Wood-chopping excursions provided discreet opportunities for study – until practical difficulties halted progress. Deft footwork was impeded by Wellington boots and I badly needed a mirror to check my posture. I therefore took to slipping away unobtrusively after washing up the supper things to the privacy of my bed cellar. There, with mirror and book to guide me, I attempted to follow the step by step manoeuvres which culminated in an illustration.

It was certainly not easy without a partner. Throwing imaginary opponents over an outstretched leg, hip or shoulder lacked conviction. Also I was concerned how to finish them off. Knocking a paratrooper to the ground might only enrage him. I therefore worked mainly on the floor in an effort to master strangleholds and locks on bones and joints. It was absorbing work which required a great deal of concentration:

"Your hold on your victim's foot can be accomplished in two ways. The orthodox hold is usually effected by grasping your own right wrist with your left hand, palm downwards, as your right hand, also palm downwards, rests upon your victim's imprisoned leg, thus forming a sort of cross lock. The stretching of your body backwards combined with the steady upward movement of your left forearm against the underpart of your victim's imprisoned leg is usually sufficient to torture your victim beyond endurance." And jolly well serve him right!

Thus it was that I found myself so engrossed in these gruesome studies during one of the secretary's evening outings that I failed to hear the telephone or the shrill cries of her old mother. It was not until an excited figure stood on the threshold of my den that our state of emergency became clear.

"What are you doing boy – lying on the floor all twisted up? Didn't you hear the phone, you noodle? That was the air raid wardens at Ottershaw! There's a light from one of our top windows shining right across the country. They think we're German spies!"

"But no one goes upstairs," I explained struggling to my feet.

"What do you know boy? I was up there myself today. You forgot to go round the building after dark and check the blackout, you noodle. They say the police will be here any moment!"

Sure enough three van loads of air raid wardens, Civil Defence and local police, all with imaginations as lurid as my own, arrived within minutes. They were convinced they had spotted signals from secret agents, and as like as not the ones who had caused an unexploded oil bomb to land in Mr Tulk's wood.

Mayhem ensued. Voices could be heard all around the building. Soon there were loud bangs on the front door – doubtless delivered with wooden rifles. The old lady was seething with a mixture of rage and panic. A seizure seemed imminent.

"Let them in boy, you great noodle! Hurry up or they'll have the door down."

"One moment," I shouted through the letter-box. "I've got about fifty keys here, and I can't find the right one."

"Let us in or we'll force an entry!"

They could hardly contain themselves. Any moment I expected the cry:

"Lay down your arms! You're completely surrounded!"

I steeled myself for the onslaught, and adopted shizenhontai. It was just one of those bitter ironies of war that I should have to test my secret skills against our own side. Unfortunately my axe and bolas were in the cellar.

Suddenly, when the moment of truth seemed inevitable, an alternative tactic presented itself.

"I think I've found the key to the side door," I bellowed. "Do you mind going round? Take the short cut through the passage to the right. You can't miss it."

There were some reluctant grumbles; and then, to my relief, I heard the shuffle of retreating footsteps across the gravel drive. The narrow unlit passage passed over the coal hole in which I stored my logs. In the excitement I had forgotten the cover was not in place. I heard a muffled shout as the first invader fell into the cavity as if it were an oubliette.

Panic engulfed his followers. The cries of fury from outside were augmented by hysterical blathering from the old woman who was dogging my footsteps.

"Now see what you've done! Just listen to them. They'll break the windows. Why don't you let them in? You've got the keys there boy. Just wait till my daughter gets back – you great noodle!"

The repetition of this expletive was beginning to rankle. Yet despite her abuse and the threatening faces pressed against the windows I kept my nerve, retained the key and finally succeeded in opening the side door.

An army of helmeted vigilantes poured in. They were led by an angry Civil Defence officer with a torn jacket and blackened face. The crescendo of accusations seemed interminable; but eventually the clamour subsided and it became embarrassingly clear that the "Chertsey spy ring" was no more than a school boy and a distraught old woman.

It was probably this incident that accelerated my return to orthodox education. In early December I was put aboard a train bound for Halifax; and from thence I was conveyed by car far beyond the wail of air raid sirens to Rishworth School perched high and remote on the summit of the Yorkshire moors.

I was sick on the train, and the long winding car journey intensified my green pallor.

"I hope you're not one of those spoon fed boys from the south," said the matron. This was the first hint of an alien culture.

She delivered me to the dormitory and left me to unpack. My luggage contained the required clothing for a minor public school and included, to my disgust, an Eton suit. But hidden amongst this pretentious attire was a small secret library of survival manuals, a well illustrated volume entitled *The Paintings of Rembrandt* and *The Art of Ju-Jitsu* by E.J. Harrison.

The Race for Supremacy

"But he ate as many as he could get," said Tweedledum.

"Eh-oop! It's a brawl!"

As the cry went up an arena of excited faces formed around us at the end of the assembly hall.

"Give over shoving," and similar colloquial cries rose above the general hubbub. Fight fans were not going to be denied free entertainment on a Monday morning.

"Scoggy and the new kid," announced a ring side commentator for the benefit of the ill-informed and the unsighted. "Let's see what he's made of."

Anything foreign presents a challenge to schoolboys; and for the Yorkshire inmates of Rishworth School my southern vowel sounds were a foreign invitation to a "brawl". The fight erupted during my first week. Combat was more akin to a wrestling bout than a bloody thumping match. It was sufficiently absorbing for spectators that prefects were loath to interfere before the bell for assembly. Having tried for three months in the cellars of the Actors' Orphanage to teach myself ju-jitsu, a fight with a real opponent was welcome fulfilment. I relished the opportunity to test my secret skills. Frank seemed to enjoy fighting as much as I did and honours were about even. It was a good introduction to a life long friendship.

"Where did you learn those tricks?" he asked later.

"It's a book I've got. I'll show you, but we must keep it to ourselves."

Frank had also been inspired by screen heroes whom he sought to emulate. Jon Hall's escape from spear throwing natives had particularly impressed him. With hands tied behind his back, this noble savage had dived into shark infested waters and swum to safety. Frank had steeled himself for a repeat performance in the changing room of the Halifax Public Swimming Baths. Rushing through astonished by-standers with hands clasped firmly behind him he had plunged head first into the pool. Unhappily he had chosen, by mistake, the shallow end, and had to be dragged out unconscious.

Our first joint venture was inspired by Baden Powell's *Scouting for Boys*. We formed an unofficial troop with a strong emphasis on outdoor pursuits, and even attempted to construct a swimming pool on the moors. An intrepid workforce dammed a stream in a declivity;

and the surface had risen nearly three feet before an enraged posse of farmers appeared over the crest of the hill. They were red faced and breathless – and by no means pleased to discover why their water supply had failed.

"You little buggers," they shouted realising from our swagger clothes that we hailed from a minor public school.

I tried to explain that once the dam was full the flow would continue uninterrupted; but this irrefutable logic delivered in an alien tongue merely incensed them further. We retreated to a safe distance and watched in sullen silence as Britain's first Dual Use Sports Facility built with voluntary labour was destroyed by vandals.

Shortly after outdoor swimming on the Pennines was nipped in the bud Britain's first School Scout Troop founded and run by the pupils was disbanded by the headmaster. He had got wind of our activities when a six foot scout staff, purchased by one affluent young enthusiast through mail order was delivered with the morning's post.

The pretext for dissolution was that our popularity was having an adverse effect on recruitment for the School Cadet Corps. It seemed there was an abundance of N.C.O.s and Officers to shout commands, but fewer and fewer foot soldiers eager to respond. I received the judgment with stoicism, and forbore to explain that marching around parade grounds in First World War puttees was a poor preparation for jungle warfare.

Disgusted with authoritarian intransigence Frank and I resorted to a secret study of my little green book – *The Art of Ju-Jitsu*. We read E.J. Harrison's historical introduction and learnt that experts call it "Judo" because it is a "way of life". Good physical condition is essential, so we undertook an heroic programme of exercise and eating.

The standard punishment for minor misdemeanours at Rishworth was running round the playground at break time under the supervision of a prefect. So by indulging in a carefully selected catalogue of petty crimes every week we insured our daily work out. The rails at the end of our beds were used for press-ups until my bed frame collapsed; and we practised chins on the bar across the top of the lavatory door.

For guidance on diet I consulted my hand book on haybox cookery.

"It says here Frank that one of the most nourishing foods you can eat is porridge oats."

"Well that'll not be hard to come by," said Frank.

Porridge was the most notorious product of the school kitchen – even lower in esteem than rock hard pastry and circular slices of meat substitute known derisively as "Walls of Jericho" and "Puncture Patches". It was thick, lumpy and unsweetened. Every boy was served a compulsory plate full as a prelude to breakfast throughout the winter; and all plates had to be returned empty.

With dedication worthy of the Japanese Samurai Frank and I launched a rescue operation. We decided to relieve our fastidious table mates of their nauseating duty.

"Just pass your plates up this end lads".

And every morning, before cornflakes came into season, eighteen plates of this repulsive "fodder" arrived at our end of the table. Long after all others had departed we remained until the last plate was scraped and the last mouthful swallowed.

Even the cook was astonished by our capacity. One morning she emerged from her lair to ask incredulously:

"You enjoy the porridge then boys?"

"Don't ever change it cook," we replied artfully. "It's wonderful how you manage it without milk or sugar." And we pressed her to describe in detail exactly how she prepared the porridge and many other grisly recipes besides. Most of them culminated with the epitaph:

"And I mixes it all up with me 'ands."

Frank was inclined to think that our unselfish heroism had its price, and suggested we make it a condition of eating other people's porridge that they donate their little rolled up pieces of bacon as well. However, on reflection, we calculated that total starvation before school might drive even the most faddy into curtailing our supplies.

Whilst I clung fairly closely to the handbook Frank experimented with a wide variety of dietary supplements. In retrospect we concluded that egg shells and blotting paper had probably contributed to his appendicitis. During his brief absence in hospital I was compelled to eat seventeen plates of porridge; and I believe this unofficial record still stands.

Thus fortified with a surfeit of food and exercise we commenced a detailed study of Chapter 3 – "Outfit Needed and Branches of Judo".

"Judo practice differs from either boxing or Western systems of wrestling in that it proceeds on the assumption that in ordinary life should one be so unfortunate as to become involved in a personal encounter one would usually be fully dressed"

"What does he mean – 'unfortunate'?" Frank asked; for encounters were our main objective. I thought it must be "irony". It was puzzling but we persevered:

"For that reason many though not all of the tricks taught necessitate hold upon portions of one's adversary's clothing. In order therefore to reproduce as far as practicable the conditions of real life the judo student wears a special costume when at work. The tunic is made of strong cotton cloth . . . the trousers also of cotton should be loose and are fastened above the hip with a running cord." So far so good. Smuggling pyjamas from the dormitory posed no problem.

The first "Branch of Judo" was headed "The Breakfall".

"In this connection I cannot too strongly impress upon the pupil the necessity for learning at the outset how to fall upon a matted floor or ground without sustaining shock or injury before he ventures to apply any sort of trick on his own account. For this purpose the novice is required to master what is known as the breakfall or method of striking the mat with the palm of either hand according to the direction in which he is falling."

"What shall we do about mats?" I said.

"Towels," said Frank.

We furtively filched a score of towels from our comrades' linen bags and spread them on the concrete floor of an unfrequented changing room. However this improvised "tatami" provided a very thin covering for such a hard surface. It did little to prevent the pain of beating concrete with bare arms. We decided to move on quickly. Skipping the remainder of Chapter 3, which dealt with posture, we turned with far more enthusiasm to Chapter 4 – "Tricks of Throwing".

At this point a series of pictures was introduced to supplement the text. Precise little pen and ink drawings, each with a title in Japanese characters, illustrated a variety of hip, leg and shoulder throws just before the point of take off. They were drawn by a Dr Shepherd who was also a black belt, and I was encouraged by this combination of art and judo. The most dramatic picture delineated the attacker on his back with "the victim" being kicked over his head.

"Throwing in a circle (TOMOENAGE) is colloquially known as the 'stomach throw'. It is quite a spectacular and drastic throw by recourse to which some comparatively small Japanese policeman in the old Yokohama 'Blood Town' has more than once rudely discomfited an obstreperous foreign 'blue jacket' looking for trouble and finding it!"

"That sounds good," said Frank, "but what's a blue jacket?"

"Can't be worse than an Eton suit!" I replied. "Let's try it."

With such lurid inspiration we practised ardently, but soon realised that one vital element of success was missing – that of surprise.

"After you have advanced a few steps he will react by trying to push you back." – Not if he's read the book too . . . We needed some unsuspecting "blue jackets". This proved to be our undoing.

We should have heeded Mr Harrison's cautionary tale about, "a celebrated expert who fell foul of a coolie in the upper room of a restaurant and promptly threw him downstairs. The coolie returned to the fray with fourteen comrades, but the expert calmly sat at the head of the stairs and as fast as the coolies came up in single file owing to the narrowness of the passage he simply choked them in detail and threw them down again. In the excitement of the moment he was rather rougher than was strictly necessary and so broke one man's neck."

Inevitably retribution followed. Excessive enthusiasm is so often misunderstood.

"The Kodokan temporarily suspended him for his conduct which was deemed unduly violent."

Frank and I were never accused of using the Rishworth stairways for similar subjugation, and not a single neck was broken; but I was certainly "deemed unduly violent". Reluctant recruits on whom we tested our progress suffered from the lack of proper mats; and "spectacular and drastic" stomach throws posed a threat to the authority of prefects who had not mastered a rolling breakfall.

Parents complained to the headmaster of malevolent practices. Aggression on the rugger field was one thing, but the mention of ju-jitsu in war time raised images of unspeakable atrocities in Japanese prisoner of war camps. The head was a strict disciplinarian and a Church of England clergyman. He abhorred any suggestion of pagan bullying. Oriental cults were anathema. Dissolution was inevitable.

I was severely reprimanded; and the first British School's Judo Club founded, organised and equipped by pupils was disbanded. (It was ten years before I founded another)

It says much for the tolerance of the Rishworth staff and their ingenuity in "chanelling the energies of youth", however maverick, that Frank and I were eventually accommodated within the system. I was placed in charge of the Junior Cadets and asked to devise their training programme. It was an unusually popular scheme which replaced marching and arms drill with activities that bore a marked resemblance to those of the disbanded Rishworth Scout Troop. An inspecting officer was impressed by its originality and made favourable comments. Frank ultimately became head boy.

However the collapse of the Rishworth judo venture might well have marked the end of my youthful fantasy but for a chance encounter many years later with a member of the Budokwai. This is the establishment recommended in *The Art of Ju-Jitsu* to "the serious student who has whet his appetite and wishes to keep in direct touch with the fountain head of inspiration for fear of being left behind in the race for supremacy."

The Moment of Truth

He took his vorpal sword in hand:
Long time the manxome foe he sought –
So rested he by the Tumtum tree,
And stood awhile in thought.

"Say Buddy, where's the nearest whore house?"

At the tender age of sixteen and fresh from a single sex school I was quite shocked to be asked for this sordid information by an American GI in the streets of Oxford; but war time emergencies had to be acknowledged even amongst the dreamy spires.

The Slade School of Art which I joined in 1943 was enjoying refuge from the London blitz in Britain's most erudite shrine. Accommodation was shared with the Ruskin School in the Ashmoleum Museum and the adjacent Food Office. In normal peace time circumstances I might have been overawed in the seat of so much learning. However the international struggle for life and death kept academic reverence in a subordinate place.

The most visible war time intrusion into Oxford was the American occupation. U.S. Army convoys clogged Cornmarket and disconsolate GIs sprawled around the pavements with loose mobile jaws.

The elegant foreign uniforms and caricature Hollywood accents were a constant peripheral reminder that elsewhere in the world people were firing live ammunition at each other with intent to kill. Far more pertinent evidence of war just around the corner was the dominant presence as mature students of British ex-servicemen. The life they had left was the one that youngsters like myself were soon to enter. Slade veterans were an odd mixture and quite unlike the cheery waving Tommies on Pathe Pictorial News.

Hugh's military fervour inevitably earned him the nickname of "Poonah". He referred to himself as "a born soldier". Premature discharge from the Army which "blighted his life" had followed the discovery of his diabetes. He had concealed the disease at his initial "medical" by scrounging some surplus urine from a healthy looking stranger and passing it off as his own.

"The finest sport of all is war," he confided to me through clouds of tobacco smoke whilst we were swimming at Tumblin Bay. (He retained his pipe even when largely submerged.) "This art game's all very well, but I should be out there fighting – with the cavalry!"

If he was sometimes confused by the introduction of tanks, and inclined to spring astride docile horses grazing in Port Meadows he was unshakable on moral principles.

"Some damned feller had the effrontery to tell me chivalry is dead. I had no option, of course, but to challenge him to a duel. Will you be my second Jerry?"

To my great disappointment the challenge was declined on the grounds of cowardice. Poonah was incredulous.

"Can you believe it? The man admitted he was a coward!"

Eddie, on the other hand, had "worked his passage" out of the Army quite deliberately by feigning madness. It was a formidable achievement to pull the wool over the eyes of professional sceptics; but nocturnal conversations with Michelangelo doggedly sustained under close scrutiny over many months did the trick.

Poor old Leo, who looked far too ill and bedraggled to be an ex-serviceman was probably invalided out. He survived in Oxford without digs by "fire-watching" every night. This voluntary duty provided a bed and nominal remuneration with which he purchased tins of baked beans. These were heated rather appropriately in a corner of the Food Office.

I sometimes saw Leo in conversation with a strange professor who sat brooding for hours in shop doorways. He had been arrested by a U.S. military policeman who presumed that anyone walking down the High Street in pyjamas must be a deserter. Despite profuse apologies when his true identity was authenticated by embarrassed college authorities the professor bore a grudge. It was always a delight to watch him stalking an unsuspecting GI, snatch the cap from his head and shout:

"Take your filthy headgear! You're a disgrace to your country and to your uniform."

Having professed he would hurl the wretched soldier's cap under a passing lorry.

Undergraduates who deferred their "call up" were only a couple of years older than myself. (Some were doing military sandwich courses which I was told had no connection with the Food Office. A pity) We saw much of these precious "Brideshead" young men on Saturday mornings when they scoured the Ashmoleum in a vain hope of acquiring unattached Slade girls. Our exotic derivations of Augustus John's Dorelia were Oxford's most prestigious prize.

"In this turbulent environment, which was as much akin to a military transit camp as to a university, I found it hard to concentrate exclusively on drawing the plaster casts of Greek gods in the Ashmoleum or the fat naked ladies in the 'life' rooms. Doryphoros and Diskobolos were a constant reminder of the need to develop my external oblique muscles." (Compared with these classical models the torso I viewed in the bedroom mirror appeared alarmingly deficient.) Life drawings aroused unexpected interest amongst GIs loitering in Beaumont Street; but I had a shrewd suspicion that offers to purchase were motivated less by an appreciation of good draughtsmanship than by an unhealthy preoccupation with nudity.

As "call-up" for war service drew close my esoteric training overshadowed "the art game". Acquisition of a fearsome book on combat at close quarters by a soldier called Fairbairn rekindled my interest in judo; but none of my new friends shared the enthusiasm of my old school mate Frank for hand to hand fighting.

"Cold steel's more in my line," said Poonah.

Years later I discovered that there was a judo club in Oxford run by a curious old man who taught his personal method under vows of secrecy to an exclusive sect – so exclusive that it certainly excluded me. I had to be content with practising rolling breakfalls under the blank gaze of the Ashmoleum plaster statues.

Mr Fairbairn (his rank escapes me) had designed a commando knife in collaboration with the brother-in-law of the Slade Professor. This tenuous connection earned me unexpected tolerance:

"Let me see what you're throwing into the Ashmoleum lawn," said Professor Schwabe. "Well you may be interested to know . . ." and I was permitted to continue practising until the point broke.

Monty's North African campaign against Rommel – "the desert fox" – was widely reported so I examined all the books by P.C. Wren available in the Public Library. *Beau Geste* and others revealed that the Foreign Legion always marched across the desert in their overcoats. It seemed the sort of training that might give me the edge in "the race for supremacy". So I undertook a series of forced marches at the height of summer similarly attired. I still have vivid memories of Blenheim Palace viewed in a state of exhaustion, soaked in sweat and in the knowledge that I still had to march eight miles back to Oxford.

For route marches, roof top ascents, trespass in Whytham Woods and other excursions I carried an axe and a coil of rope as unobtrusively as possible. Poonah was very impressed by the seriousness of my approach and assured me that when I entered the Army it would all stand me in good stead.

"They'll be watching you from the moment you step inside."

I drank six pints of water a day (sometimes, for fear I'd forgotten, at one draught), reread Peter Fleming's *Brazilian Adventure*, and lest the war should spread to the Matto Grosso practised canoeing on the

Cherwell. Oxford was so thoroughly saturated with poseurs, cranks and genuine eccentrics that my comparatively modest idiosyncrasies passed largely unnoticed; which was probably just as well. Even when I conspired with a vegetarian called John Walton to barricade the entire Oxford Union in their debating chamber I escaped detection. My contribution was to fell a small tree with which to jam the exit doors. Whilst making my escape through the crowds outside a heavy disguise worthy of Sherlock Holmes concealed my identity. It was a useful trial run. Unaware of the Cambridge monopoly I could not exclude the possibility of transference to MI5.

Failure to obtain personal instruction in the diverse skills I had explored did not deter me. I was confident that modern army training would make good this deficiency. It was a naive assumption which could not have been more mistaken.

Victory in Europe was celebrated by dancing late into the night on Magdalene Bridge. Two weeks later I was "called up" to the Army Barracks at Richmond Yorkshire, and made the long journey north convinced that "the moment of truth" had arrived. The barbarity of our remaining enemies persuaded me to set aside the first stirrings of conscientious misgiving and enter the fray wholeheartedly. Now that we had defeated Hitler I was curious to discover how my years of improvised amateur training would compare with the Army's professional prescription for fighting a nation of judo experts.

During my short stay at Richmond we were subjected to a personal selection procedure. It was a dispiriting anti-climax. The tests confirmed my I.Q. and incompetence with machinery. Without the handicap of an overcoat I completed the five mile walk in a record time, but there was no opportunity to demonstrate ability in hand to hand combat. They failed to identify my knowledge of how to fell a man with a match box, burst his eardrums with a clap of the hands and tie him to a tree by his legs. I was bitterly disillusioned and entered the subsequent interview with a Personal Selection Officer determined to serve my time as a cook. At least I could then be sure of eating enough porridge. However my school record appeared to preclude such menial service.

"Now look here Hicks, you've been to a good school, played rugger and that sort of thing. Outstanding service in the Cadet Corps. Why on earth should you wish to become a cook? Good Lord! We can ensure you get enough to eat! I think you should try for a commission."

My platoon commander at Sandhurst, who sported a white Alsatian dog, found me difficult to categorise. He was impressed by my unorthodox tactics in simulated warfare, unaware of their origin in Baden Powell's defence of Mafeking. On the other hand he was irritated by my "unsoldierly bearing" and the initiation of a round of applause for the Regimental Band's rendering of selections from "Show Boat" during Dinner Night. This was an appalling gaffe!

The benefit of my forced marches to Woodstock tipped the balance. Ability to shout orders and encouragement when all others were breathless with exhaustion marked me as a natural leader, and I "passed out" with an "above average" grade. The Sword of Honour was awarded to an ex-Coldstream Guards sergeant major who had lost one and a half testicles to a German bullet. He could never disguise his contempt for my idiosyncratic successes and monumental appetite.

Peace broke out before I was commissioned, so life as a young subaltern in Monty's Modern Army at Lancaster's Bowerham Barracks was robbed of warlike purpose. Old soldiers reminisced, Demster constantly apologised for the leaking silver tea pot and zeal was replaced by the universal search for "a cushy number".

"Always carry papers old boy if you're sloping off. It looks purposeful," one old hand advised.

I exploited my appointment as Sports Officer by training intensively for five different sports; and on volunteering for the duty of Messing Officer I contrived on Dinner Nights the only nine course meals my brother officers had ever encountered. The C.O. at first suspected that the abundance of cutlery was one of Jerry's little jokes, but as the splendour of the first banquet unfolded suspicion gave way to ecstasy. All present were sworn to secrecy:

"It would not do, gentlemen, in times of rationing for these remarkable occasions to be spoken of outside the mess. I trust that I can count on your discretion."

Less conventional excitement in this decadent routine was mainly of my own creation. Fortunately the disguise I assumed as a fictitious Colonel Foley, who made a surprise inspection of our unit, was never uncovered by Army Security; and the unhappy incident in which a cloud of poisonous gas descended on Lancaster "passed over" without casualties. My final departure in "a blaze of glory" was entirely unintentional. The unexpected sequence of events which ignited the barracks during my homeward journey was the sort of accident which might happen to almost anyone. I did not hear of it until long after when I was told the C.O.'s wife said, "He was such a nice young man. I'm sure he never meant to set our barracks on fire."

However the most curious aspect of my somewhat bizarre period of military service was the omission of any form of instruction in unarmed combat. I had often seen it in films depicting army training; but neither as a recruit, cadet nor officer did I encounter anyone who had fought the enemy hand to hand or had the slightest idea of how to set about it. My requests for judo instruction seemed to be an embarrassment. They produced evasive glances, excessive explanations or even downright tetchy belligerence. Any expectations I had harboured that the Army would abound in heroic stealthy warriors privy to the most deadly fighting skills were entirely extinguished.

I learned how to strip a Bren gun, give the word of command on the correct foot, mount a bicycle by numbers and pass the port to the left. But I returned to "civy street" with no more knowledge of hand to hand fighting than I had gleaned in my school days from E.J. Harrison's book.

It was, therefore, with little thought of judo or any other sport that I rejoined the Slade once more in its home at University College London. I was happy to set rugger behind me having had a surfeit of bar room coaching and charabanc trips enlivened with communal singing about "My Little Sister Lily's" appalling family and sanitary arrangements at Mobile. Yukio Tani as a fount of inspiration was transcended by Rembrandt, the Impressionists, Sickert, and Picasso. I had become a serious artist.

And yet . . . and yet . . . the thirst for physical excitement was not so easily slaked. I was bursting with fitness without purpose. Chanting in unison at UCL rags was spurned by the Slade ex-servicemen. I tried to diffuse my energy and economise on tube fares by running round London barefoot. It kept me fit but lacked excitement. Traffic was not so dense in 1948.

During my service years Poonah had gone to earth in Chagford, Leo had been expelled for defacing a painting by a follower of the Pre-Raphaelites and Eddie had become an international Neo-Dada celebrity. Only John Walton remained to assist my rehabilitation. He began by introducing me to Anne – my future wife.

John also remembered the restlessness of my Oxford persona and observed that it had not subsided. One day he said, "There's someone I think you ought to meet," and he led me to the Chemistry Department's basement where the glass blowers operated. He singled out a man who was dexterously manipulating a red hot glass tube and introduced us:

"Jerry Hicks meet Jim Frost. Jerry's always been interested in judo, and I'm told, Jim, that you're a black belt."

That was John's second introduction that changed my life.

The Budokwai

Then she found herself at last in the beautiful garden among the bright flowers and the cool fountains.

Jim Frost's vision of judo matched my needs exactly. He discussed it unpretentiously in his workshop at University College London.

His small team of glass blowers invented and constructed apparatus for the Chemistry Department immediately behind the Slade where I spent my days drawing and painting.

Concise Cockney chatter flowed from Jim whilst he worked; and, working alongside him, his minute assistant scrambled on and off her stool. Comments were punctuated by the infusion of breath into molten glass. A word or two – a twirl and a puff – a few more words, a jet of flame, a final puff – and the glowing globules were coaxed into precise orderly shapes. The man was an artist and like many good artists he made creation look easy – almost casual.

"My own club's the Budokwai – you've heard of it! That's right, Tani used to teach there – a really rough handful he was – used to put his head in your belly and ram you against the wall – just to see what you'd do! Well you didn't know what to do did you – so he got you to try it on him, and he just slithered down the wall!

"Tani taught Leggett and he's something special – the only non Japanese 5th dan. He doesn't compete since his stroke, but he can still handle the best in the club – very intellectual man, runs the B.B.C. Japanese section – good pianist I believe, a degree in Law and a Zen Buddhist! No, you don't have to be a Buddhist to do judo – some of them take up Zen like old Christmas Humphreys – and some get a bit carried away like Shaw Desmond – he's a laugh! Yeah, a few of them are keen on self defence – looks good in displays – if it doesn't go wrong! But in real life I keep out of trouble, I'm a pacifist. Most of us do judo because we like it. It sort of gets you – the fanatics give up work if it interferes with their judo! – The Budokwai's run by G.K. – that's what we call him – his name's Gungi Koizumi – founded the club years ago. Yeah, that's right 1918! How did you know that? Oh, I think you'd better come along – but you ought to do a bit first. I don't do much myself nowadays, but if you want to organise a college club – find some mats and a few bodies – I'll do the instruction – better wear some old clothes . . ." and that's exactly what happened.

A week or so later a handful of eager young men dressed like tramps spread a miserable selection of coir mats on the UCL lawn. As a spectacle for passing academics, beadles and Gower Street pedestrians our tatty little assembly was bracketed with the Morris Dancers.

Jim's arrival bestowed credibility. He sauntered out in authentic judo-gi, and simultaneously stepped out of his zori, knotted his black belt without a downward glance and commenced a chatty introduction.

The instruction followed an abbreviated version of E.J. Harrison's book *The Art of Ju-Jitsu*. By Jim's standards this was fairly orthodox; but he concluded the session with some free practice called "randori". I seized the first opportunity to fight with Jim – and judo came to life. Moves which hitherto had seemed complex and cumbersome merged into a fluid pattern of movement, and I became caught up in his rhythm. Jim chatted away as if he were still blowing glass:

"You're doing all right then – not much good at throws myself – prefer groundwork – Here! Who showed you that? – Try it again, but pull a bit more with your left hand – Oh! – Getting serious are we? . . . You all right then?"

The last remark was made as he patted my cheeks encouragingly. I'd stumbled him to the ground and tried for a hold. His neck lock was on before I sensed danger. It was the first time I'd been rendered unconscious.

"Sorry about that," said Jim. "You're supposed to tap before you pass out – but never mind, you did well – quite a handful."

John Goldsmith watched our weekly sessions on the lawn with delight. He joined the Slade as a porter, having previously worked in Billingsgate Market as a porter. He probably assumed the jobs were similar. A rugged background in a family of professional pugilists left him thirsting for beer and punch-ups.

He recognised me as an ally.

"When those Engineers come over 'ere to try and nick our gramophone we don't need no 'elp Jerry boy. You and I can take the lot on the stairs. They can only come at us two at a time."

It was an exciting idea. I was reminded of the expert in Japan who strangled fourteen coolies on a stairway. But when the invaders were confronted with John and me in position Anne invited them all to join our "hop", and the evening passed off without a single blow or strangulation.

However the next day John had a little excitement when Scotland Yard detectives located the priceless Turkish carpet I'd "transferred" from elsewhere in the college to our sitting out room.

"I guessed you'd nicked it Jerry boy when it took four of 'em to carry it back – but I never let on."

Whilst John and I failed to become comrades in arms (much to his regret) my weekly judo battles with Jim forged a close rapport; and he proved a most resourceful friend. When the artist John Minton responded facetiously to an invitation to talk to the Slade Society by requesting a bottle of gin and a bomb I turned to Jim for the bomb.

"No problem," he said. "What you want is a nice little bang with no damage caused."

To Minton's astonishment that's exactly what he got. If anyone asked him how his lecture went there could have been only one answer . . .

Soon after the bomb Jim invited me to the Budokwai. I tried to express appreciation without betraying my awe. The address in E.J.Harrison's book had been familiar for years, but I had never expected to cross the threshold of Europe's oldest judo club. As we travelled to Victoria by bus I remembered Shaw Desmond's lurid account of being sprung upon by a ferocious Japanese uttering an uncanny scream the moment he entered the dojo. Mr Desmond claimed to have used this scream (called "kiai") to fell an athlete at 20 paces. I also recalled the story of a man concealed behind the entrance of an opium den in Limehouse. He whacked new comers on the shins with a pick axe handle to test their reactions and fighting spirit.

This caused me a little apprehension as I was still rather sore after falling from a tree. I'd been sketching in Regent's Park Zoo and, fired with enthusiasm for the agility of the gibbons, the temptation of an overhanging branch had overwhelmed my sense of propriety. Anne had watched in astonishment as I disappeared into the foliage to reappear an instant later plummeting to the ground head first. In addition to a few abrasions the hand which had protected my head now boasted a bandaged finger.

A small shopfront behind Buckingham Palace discreetly displayed the Budokwai title. No external clues as to the nature of Budo were evident. As we entered I glanced nervously behind the door, before descending narrow stairs to the changing room. "No Smoking" notices were reassuring. In a subdued atmosphere (very different from a rugby pavilion) I gently eased myself into a jacket recently acquired from the Mombasa Ju-Jitsu Association. It was made of coarse sail cloth which gave me a marginal advantage. If opponents tugged at it too vigorously it tore the skin off their knuckles.

We crept through a darkened lower dojo where I could just discern a solitary figure standing on his head. A light in the upper dojo revealed a small black belted instructor, not unlike Mr Moto, concluding some private tuition in self defence. His obese middle aged pupil looked as though the nearest he would come to a rough house would be jostling for service in a lounge bar. He parried a couple of delicate blows as instructed, glanced at Jim and me with ill-disguised alarm and left hurriedly.

"Your jacket's dirty Frost," growled Moto as he stalked out without springing on me. Jim made a jocular reply and then said to me in a lower tone:

"That's G.K.'s son-in-law."

Early arrivals began to enter. Amongst their orthodox judo clothing my Mombassa seemed rather uncouth. They bowed towards the wall to wall mats and sat silently on the tightly stretched canvas cover. It was certainly a vastly superior surface to towels on concrete or coir mats on grass. My eyes strayed upwards to photographs of an elderly Japanese demonstrating throws; they were covered with diagrammatic arrows.

At length one or two couples wearing coloured belts braved the tranquillity and began to grapple on the mats. Their occasional kiai screams violated the silence but failed to fell surrounding practitioners. An overweight brown belt approached me and said:

"Would you care for a little randori?"

Jim nodded reassuringly and I sprang to my feet. The brown belt took hold of my Mombassa so condescendingly that I was tempted to render him unconscious by clapping his ears; but I contented myself with seizing him vigorously and launching a few preliminary kicks.

"DO you mind?" he yelped rhetorically. "You're grasping my flesh."

I adjusted my hold deferentially. His exaggerated threat to my left side was a transparent feint and I evaded the right attack when it eventually came. Having apparently shot his only bolt he bowed and said a little grudgingly:

"You've got a good defence."

Jim whispered, "Come and have a go with 'Kid' Gregory."

Kid was a blue belt (one grade below brown) but built like a fighting man. After a few tentative exchanges he gave my Mombassa an enormous tug, and I had an instant to recognise the entry for hane-goshi – "one of the prettiest throws in the entire judo repertoire" according to E.J.Harrison. I shot upwards like a Champagne cork. Kid's control of my landing made a clumsy breakfall superfluous. He glanced ruefully at his knuckles, then threw me twice more before I got my leg behind his and brought us both to the ground.

Later under the showers Kid said he hoped to win his black belt within a few months. If the loose skinned brown belt characterised the opposition it seemed a realistic goal. Then he intended to abandon commercial art for full time judo training in Japan. I was awed.

Before I left the dojo Jim said, "Ask Peter Foster for a practice."

A black belt with a Mexican moustache and a handkerchief tied round his neck was sitting cross-legged in the corner. He responded to my request by standing up and looking at the clock. I thought he might have a train to catch. After knocking my feet from under me with a foot technique he threw me five times with harai-goshi. I anticipated the third and grabbed his waist which caused an untidy landing. Foster spoke for the first time:

"If you hang on I'll fall on you."

The fourth time I hung on, and he fell on me. The fifth time I let go. He seemed satisfied, glanced at the clock, bowed and returned silently to his corner.

I watched two more victims fall five times each to Foster's harai-goshi between time checks. The throw was crisp, spectacular and much simpler than E.J.Harrison's description. I wondered how much training commitment was necessary to acquire similar skill and had a nagging suspicion that I was going to find out.

As we made our departure through the late arrivals in the entrance lobby the reverential spell of the dojo was less pervasive. Men were speaking at normal volume. Jim said:

"I'll introduce you to G.K." and I was confronted by the Japanese in the photographs.

"What have you done to your hand?" the old gentleman inquired with a friendly smile.

I hesitated, not wishing to appear irrational.

"I sort of fell on it." He massaged the joint for a few minutes and it felt looser.

"You must learn to take a fall," he said.

During the return bus journey I explained the ridiculous cause of my injury and Jim said:

"You should have told the old man. He's got a great sense of humour."

I must have looked sceptical for he elaborated:

"Last week a lad asked him to translate a Japanese inscription on some judo trousers. The old man put on his specs and said completely dead pan, 'Stolen from the Budokwai'!"

We laughed unrestrainedly in the front of the bus. Rain streaked the windows and I wondered if washing my Mombassa would destroy its cutting edge. Eleven eventful years had elapsed since E.J.Harrison's book had first aroused my curiosity about judo; and now I had fought in the Budokwai. If the thought crossed my mind that penetrating beneath the chameleon skin of this foreign culture would be a little more complex than learning how to throw people on their backs (and that I might still be involved when I was as old as G.K.) it didn't trouble me. Harai-goshi was enough to be going on with.

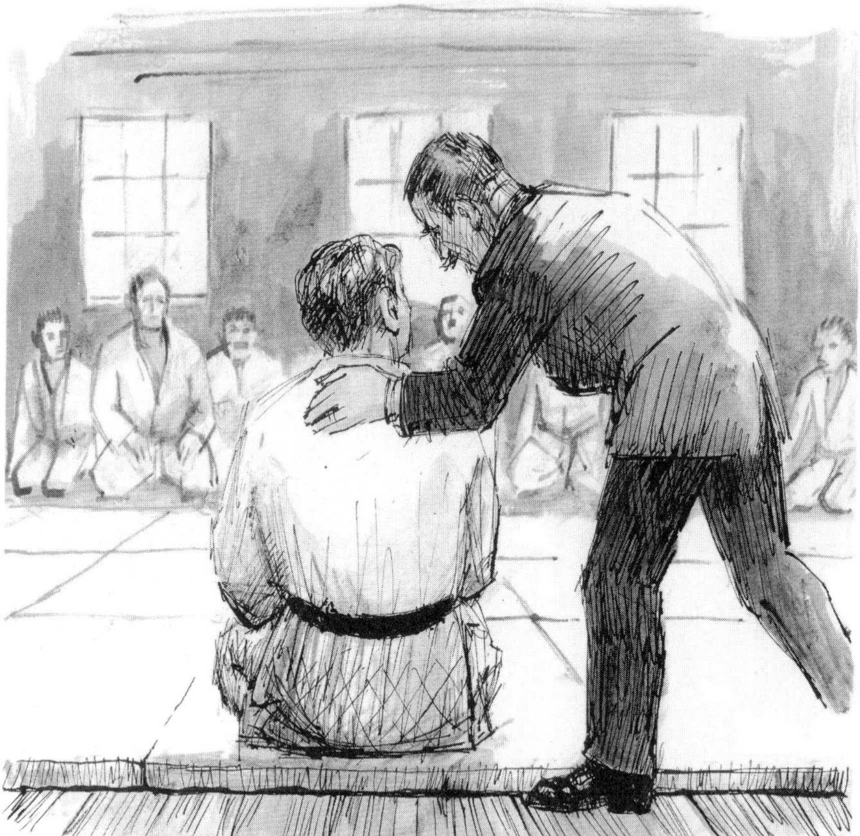

The Coveted Black Belt

*"Well, this is good!" said Alice. "I never expected
I should be a Queen so soon."*

The first award of a black belt, or dan grade, in the west of England was made posthumously to a member of Judokwai Bristol called Bob Taylor. This unique honour was in recognition of his heroism in pursuing two armed bank robbers. One turned and shot him dead at point blank range. Both robbers were hanged.

On moving from London to Bristol to take up a teaching appointment in 1951, I seized the first opportunity to visit Bob Taylor's club. I climbed the concrete stairs of a suburban athletic pavilion, and discovered a lugubrious handful of judo men spreading ten lumpy agility mattresses, which were then covered with a loose canvas, on the floor. The surface was more reminiscent of my schoolboy improvisations than the authentic tatami on which I had trained in London. I was anxious that my toes might be caught in the canvas.

The senior grade in evidence was a green belt who was at pains to assure me that a blue belt sometimes visited. Whilst fastening my comparatively modest orange belt, his oblique questions revealed that I hailed from the Budokwai, Britain's oldest and most revered judo club. Immediately my status was inflated.

"Would you care for a little Butsukari?" he inquired when we had completed some perfunctory stretching. It sounded like an invitation to afternoon tea.

As we engaged in the ritual repetition of uncompleted throws, an orange belt (who, I was told in confidence, practised hypnotism) was severely critical of my harai-goshi. After demonstrating the correct method, he invited me to compete with him in randori.

"What was that?" he grunted with some asperity, after I dumped him with my only throw.

"Harai-goshi," I replied, and the green belt explained:

"He's from the Budokwai."

As the one eyed leader of the blind, I soon found myself elected onto the committee and requested to advise on all aspects of technique and club organisation. Acutely aware of my own technical limitations, I suggested spending their jealously hoarded funds on engaging London instructors. Thus Judokwai Bristol, albeit a little reluctantly, began to raise its sights.

Geof Gleeson paid a visit shortly before he abandoned aeronautical engineering for full time judo training in Japan; and Iain Morris, who wore the latest nylon socks and travelled to the most far flung judo outposts with little more than judo-gi and a toothbrush, ran two grading examinations. He promoted me first to blue and then to brown belt. Over supper, on the second occasion, I mentioned to Iain my interest in painting a portrait of Gungi Koizimi – the founder of the Budokwai; and some months later he made the necessary arrangements.

During a series of sittings at "G.K.'s" home in Ebury Street, I formed a close friendship with "the father of British judo". I was enormously impressed by the energetic and idealistic way in which he promoted judo around the country, and was interested to learn that he had personally established Judokwai Bristol. His anecdotes about the diverse responses to his pioneering crusade and his Oriental appearance were very amusing. Whilst walking in the Derbyshire Dales he was assailed by a farmer who pressed him to visit his home:

"My wife has never seen a Japanese!"

The portrait pleased G.K. We both signed it – to confer authenticity; and he proposed that I present it to the Budokwai when their new extensive premises were formally opened in Kensington. It still hangs alongside a painting of Yukio Tani – the Budokwai's first instructor.

These renewed links with the Budokwai enabled me to arrange a series of courses for Judokwai Bristol by the best teachers in the country. G.K. epitomised the club's image of a benign oriental sensei; and he distilled into a week his personal vision of "the gentle way". I felt particularly honoured when Trevor Leggett offered to run a further course. His 5th dan was the highest grade held by a non Japanese in the world, and usually he restricted his teaching to a select number of elite competitors. His scholarly, Zen approach to skill and tactics made a profound impression on us all; and he persuaded me that a black belt was within my grasp, if I could manage regular weekend training in London.

A black belt! I had been told not to ask questions before I was a black belt, and that when I was, I would not need to. It seemed a "cop out", but certainly indicated the enormous prestige of "the coveted black belt". Anne was very supportive of the travelling commitment and smell of embrocation I sustained for the next two years.

Towards the end of this period, Geof Gleeson returned from Japan as a 4th dan and infused an enormous sense of purpose into the

Budokwai. He captained the first British team to become the European Champions; and his uncompromising approach accepted no excuses from them – or me!

"Don't worry about the blood. If you keep your head up, it won't get split open again. Clean up quickly or you'll stain the mats. The trouble with this lot is they think judo's a game for bloody old women!"

I was pleased to be excluded from "this lot", and thereafter restricted my randori to the hard men: Charlie Mack, whose broken toes alarmed a shoe shop assistant who viewed the carnage through an X-ray fitting machine: Tommy McDermot, who never let such trifles as cracked ribs disrupt his training – I can still hear his raucous cry after a two and a half hour sweat session, as we all staggered lifeless from the mats, "Somebody's using too much strength": and a handful of rugged fighting men who left me covered with sticking plaster from twelve separate injuries. They taught me much – not least survival.

On my third attempt at a dan grading exam, and after much help from Geof, I scored eight ippons to win five contests against brown belts and a draw against a black belt. One win was against the rising young star, Syd Hoare, who won all his other contests. So I was guardedly optimistic the following week when Syd told me a black belt had been tied round his judo-gi.

Optimism gave way to alarm, with the premature disclosure of my success in the west country press. I feared it would invalidate the award. However, the announcement had been made by Leggett, who prophesied consequential benefits to the region.

Written confirmation finally arrived, and Eddie Beach, the chairman and oldest member of the Judokwai, spoke of "this great honour" in such awed tones that the club began talking in whispers. An article in the *Bristol Evening Post*, entitled "The Judo Gyms of Cotham Grammar School" provoked some elderly colleagues to complain of "infra dig" publicity; but the Head was delighted.

Mindful of Leggett's prophesy, our recently formed Western Area Judo Association invited me to undertake a promotional tour of our region – a shrewd move to assert the pre-eminence of the British Judo Association for which G.K. had gained international accreditation; but it placed a heavier responsibility on me than I expected.

Before undertaking the tour, my grade was registered with the Kodokan in Japan, and I undertook instruction in secret resuscitation methods called Katsu. Following a session at the Budokwai, Syd Hoare, John Newman, half a dozen other new black belts and I awaited Leggett's arrival with apprehension. It was heightened when he advised us to use the toilet. Having explained the occasional necessity for reviving victims from unconsciousness, he demonstrated two methods under a pledge of secrecy.

John and I were paired, and alternately rendered unconscious – a genuine subject on which the other could practise his chosen method. Neither of us needed help. It was the first time any of the group had submitted to strangulation without a fight. None found it easy.

Later I was told G.K. lightened his Katsu instruction with a little joke:

"Katsu will also revive victim from the dead. If I may have one volunteer to be killed, I will revive him."

My tour encompassed Weston, Bridgwater, Taunton, Exeter and St. Austell. Sessions followed the familiar routine of warm-up, instruction, grading exam and free practice, when the adventurous could test their skills against the new black belt. Such was the wearer's aura, that, even in the general mêlée, it would have been a profound shock if I had been thrown. Furthermore my own attacks were expected to succeed effortlessly every time.

"I wasn't all that impressed. Old George had him worried for a moment with his drop tai-otoshi; and he missed his first attack against Eric."

"That was a feint, wasn't it?"

"Come on! If you're a black belt, you don't need to feint. You just throw 'em. No. He definitely used too much strength with his uchi-mata, It could do you a mischief."

"Quite effective on the ground though."

"What do you expect? He's a black belt."

Such were the comments from the changing room experts which were occasionally reported back.

I was driven from Exeter to St. Austell by the west's elder statesman, Major John Bricknell.

"I'd like you to make a specially good impression on our Cornish friends," said John, beaming through his monocle. "They've somehow got mixed up with a dissident organisation – very active in Cornwall, I believe. We really could do with bringing them into the BJA. Some of these jokers are awarding their own dan grades and making a mockery of the whole system. It's up to you to show them what a black belt really is."

"What about the Cornish wrestlers, John? Do any of them try their hand at judo?"

"No. I'm sure they stick to their own thing. It's only the idiot fringe we have to worry about."

The St. Austell club greeted us with the guarded courtesy their ancestors reserved for the Customs Officers. "A bunch of wreckers" was my private assessment of the sidelong glances directed towards my new black belt.

When everyone seemed to be on the mats, I clapped my hands to indicate I was ready to start the session. There was no response. A group of officials surrounded John, and those on the mats appeared to be awaiting the outcome.

Presently John approached me in his most avuncular way.

"I rather think, Jerry, that they would prefer to start with a little activity. Not to put too fine a point on it, they aren't interested in your instruction until they've seen you in action."

"OK John. What do they want me to do?"

"They want you to take on the whole club."

I took a deep breath, and adjusted my belt for reassurance.

"Right-ho John. Line 'em up!"

About twenty assorted coloured belts, including brown, knelt down in no special order facing me. We all bowed. As we stood someone pushed the first wrecker towards me. I did a little bounce, eased back my collar Gleeson style and we were off.

They didn't give anything away, but there was no difficulty in popping them over with my limited repertoire. After half a dozen, when I had just decided it wasn't going to be so bad after all, John beckoned me to the mat side.

"Watch out for the Cornish Wrestling Champion," he whispered. "The big feller." There were at least four big ones to come.

A tall man took hold with disarming casualness. He couldn't conceal his fast response when I feinted an attack. Yet when I threw him twice with sasae-tsuri-komi-ashi, he flew. Perhaps it was the wrong guy. Yet his demeanour was clearly intended to signal, "Relax. I'm not going to attack you."

If I hadn't been waiting for the "Fool's mate", his big gun would have buried me. I made the evasion look easier than it was, and said, "Well tried."

Suddenly the tension eased. The remainder of the line came out smiling, and we had a bit of fun – genuine randori. When they'd all had a go we knelt and bowed. The wrestler nodded to the administrators who approached John and said:

"All right, we'll join. How much?"

As we drove back in John's new Jaguar, over Bodmin Moor and past Jamaica Inn, he chuckled. They'd been happy to part with the registration fee, we'd run a BJA grading exam and the wrestler,

Keith Menadue, had been awarded a well deserved brown belt. John said:

"Taunton have planned a display and Area Dinner. They want to make a special presentation to you as guest of honour; and very well deserved, if I may say so."

Anne and I travelled to the event well wrapped up for winter. I was wearing an army surplus beaver skin hat which had cost five shillings. After dinner the chairman presented me with a judo suit on which his wife had embroidered the nearest Japanese equivalent to my name – Hikosu.

It was not until we arrived home in Bristol, that I discovered the loss of my hat. I rang Taunton to see if it had been left in the Town Hall. Nothing had been reported as found, but they'd inquire – immediately.

Shortly after 3 a.m. we were awakened by three rings on our door bell. I lurched downstairs in my night clothes, and was astonished to discover a police motor cyclist on the doorstep. He handed me my hat.

"We were told it was top priority, Sir. We understand you're a black belt."

Nowadays any serious judo player expects to obtain at least a 1st dan black belt. In a good session Judokwai Bristol boasts over a dozen black belts up to 6th dan on the mats. The necessary wins in a competitive exam for dan grades no longer have to be accomplished in one session; points can be accumulated over a number of events. Katsu is no longer taught. Black belts are thrown by good coloured belts in clubs all over the country every night of the week. Judo has changed.

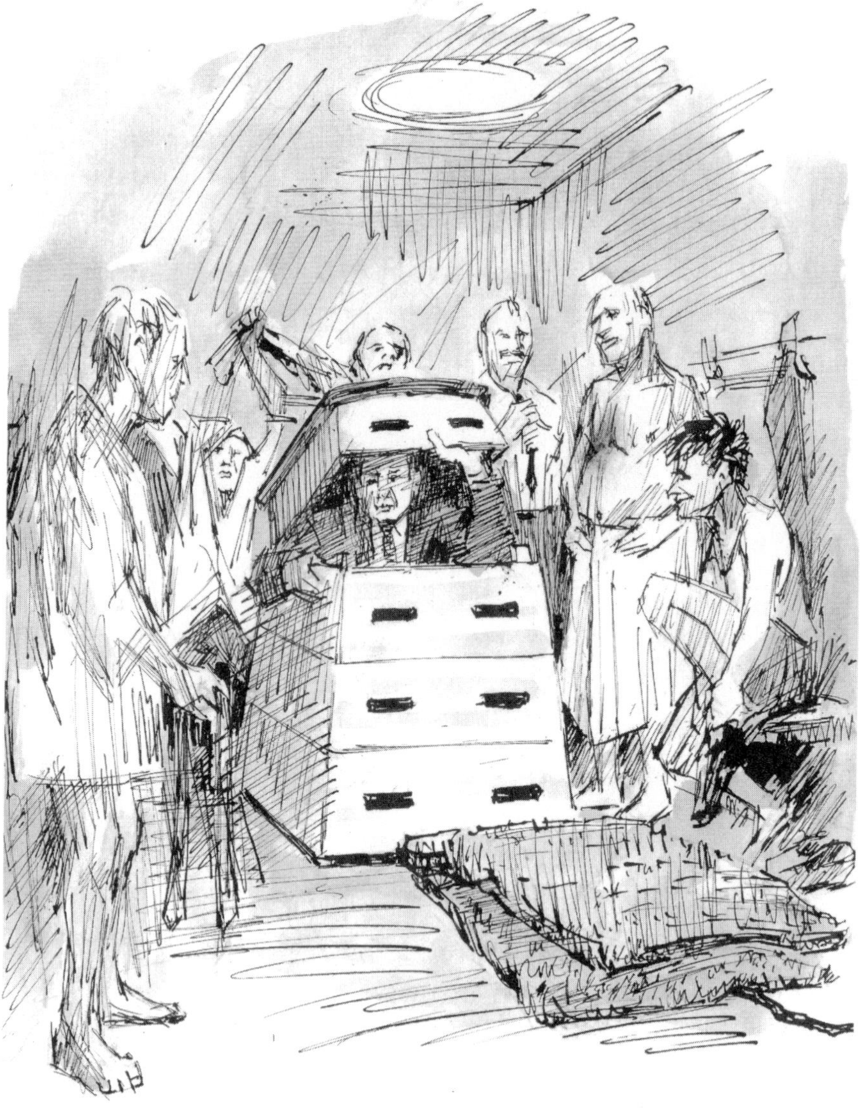

The Wooden Horse

*"There might be some sense in your knocking,"
the Footman went on, without attending to her,
"if we had the door between us. For instance,
if you were inside you might knock, and I could
let you out, you know."*

In the early postwar years, The Central Council of Physical Recreation took THE WORD OF SPORT like a great crusade to those accustomed to enjoying games without changing their clothes. Evangelical demonstrations of Yoga, Medau, Epee, Judo and other emerging sports were given at fêtes, festivals, galas and outings. We performed our obscure rites during intervals at football matches and over coffee after reunion dinners. The incredulous audiences seemed startled by our athletic skills. They were certainly embarrassed by our curious clothing. It was as if the cast of the Mikado had entered a pub, wearing full regalia, in order to recruit for the chorus.

Evening class advertisements were more reassuring. If my own sport of Judo appeared on the same page as Joinery and required nothing more elaborate than "an old jacket", perhaps it wasn't so remote after all. Braver spirits enlisted, regardless of aptitude, and on the first night many removed ties and rolled up sleeves with bravado. However, few could disguise the intimidating effect on them of the changing room . . . embrocation and cold showers were an alien culture . . . a far cry from being sewn in for the winter and not weakening the back with washing. Ritual changing of clothing two or three times a day has always been a preoccupation of the upper classes.

It wasn't unknown in rural districts for orthodox judo kit to be pulled over street clothes – on one occassion without removing shoes! Socks were always a major embarrassment. Would strangers notice the hole in the heel? This was unlikely since most of the group were absorbed in surreptitiously rubbing away the grime from between their toes with lick and loo paper.

When the awful truth, that trousers had to be changed for judo, was revealed a disturbing problem was posed. What should be worn underneath? Covert glances at the instructor sought to unravel the mystery. Did he wear underpants, jock strap, or the exotic Japanese fundoshi? Was it safe without a box?

As the instructor at Bristol's first Evening Institute Judo Class, I sought to escape this tension by availing myself of a separate changing room. It also seemed a wise precaution in view of the recent theft of a pair of socks. On emerging, brown belted, from my isolation I disregarded the unusual attire of my class with studied nonchalance, and persuaded the timid to shed their shoes and step onto the mats.

One such reluctant pupil lost the entire sleeve of his old sports jacket when I gave it a sharp tug. This technical manoeuvre called "tskuri" had never achieved such dramatic results before. Without betraying my surprise I changed to the left hand grip. Another sharp tug immediately detached the other sleeve.

He looked worried.

"Don't worry on my account. I shall practise the collar hold."

He showed increased signs of alarm.

"What's the matter?" I said. "This is an 'old' jacket isn't it?"

He shook his head unbelievingly.

"No, its my best jacket. I only looked in to see what all the banging was about."

Unfortunately, their apprehension about changing rooms proved justified.

At the end of one session a pupil came to my room in distress and announced that his entire wage packet had been stolen from his pocket. The damage was more than financial. How could he explain unguarded trousers to his wife?

I also suspected an undertone of challenge: "You're a bloody black belt aren't you?" (all instructors were black belts to novices) "Let's see your ju-jitsu sort this one out." That was the message in his eyes.

"This is a very serious matter," I said with quiet authority. "You must report it at once to the local Police Station."

The judo class was held in Cotham Grammar School at which I taught art during the day. The following morning I was summoned from the art room at the request of a police officer.

"Inspector Chivers. You'll remember the name because of the jellies."

"You've come about the theft at the judo class?" I said.

"We've got to put a stop to this, haven't we?"

"Well yes . . ."

"We must apprehend the criminal."

I was impressed. No prevarication. Straight to the heart of the matter.

"But how do you propose to catch him Inspector?" I was beginning to sound like Dr Watson.

"I shall depend on you to find somewhere for me to maintain observation. He'll strike again." He was beginning to sound like Sherlock Holmes.

"I'll do my best," I said, rising modestly to the occasion.

"Then until this time tomorrow, sir."

I almost expected him to brush past Professor Moriarty on the way out.

After careful consideration I devised two alternative plans; but my mounting enthusiasm received a severe jolt when Inspector Chivers burst into the school foyer at the appointed hour. He was in a state of extreme agitation and pointed distractedly at his torn dishevelled trousers.

"Look at that! Just look at the state of my trousers. A cat did that! Brought me off my bike and buckled the wheel. What are they going to say at the station? I'll get the sack!"

"How very unfortunate," I ventured.

"Unfortunate!" he shouted. Children were peering excitedly through classroom windows. "I should say it's unfortunate . . . but I saw where the cat came from. I proceeded to the house and found a child sitting on the stairs, pretending to be innocent. She didn't know who I was, mind. I said, 'That cat should be kept under proper control!' That shook her."

"I've found somewhere for you to keep observation." I was anxious lest he should lose his sense of purpose.

"Well let's have a look," he replied with some return of the old Chivers.

I indicated a cupboard overlooking the changing room entrance; and, alternatively, a trap door letting onto a flat roof above the room itself. He found the cupboard too remote from the scene of the crime, and the flat roof too exposed to the onset of inclement weather. I felt rather downcast.

"You'll have to do better than that, sir," he said with fatherly reproof. Sherlock Holmes was back in command. "I'll be in again on Monday."

Over the weekend I went to see a film called *The Wooden Horse*; and it inspired a brain wave.

"Right, Inspector Chivers," I said, after inquiring about his bicycle. "I've planned the perfect trap. The changing room is sometimes used to store gymnastic equipment. On Thursday it will contain the Wooden Horse! It is, in fact, a gymnastic box, and from inside you'll be able to command a clear view of the changing room through the holes used as handgrips. If the thief strikes, you will press a switch, linked by electric cable under agility mats, to a light bulb in the gym. The light will be under the continuous surveillance of my assistant; and should it be activated he will inform me. Within seconds the changing room will be surrounded by judo men dressed for action. How's that?"

He did not betray any excitement.

"Won't it be uncomfortable in the box?"

"I can provide cushions."

"Yes, we'll certainly need cushions." His control was impressive.

"The class starts at seven thirty. They begin to arrive at seven fifteen. I'll expect you at seven," I said.

When the first pupils entered the changing room everything was in position – The Wooden Horse, wire cleverly concealed under the mats, a light attached to the wall bars in the gym – everything except Inspector Chivers. At seven twenty he arrived.

"It's too late Inspector," I snapped, glancing at his trousers. "Some of them are here already."

His eyes narrowed as he scanned the group. "They look honest enough lads . . . we'll go ahead."

"Aren't you supposed to suspect everybody?" I whispered as he climbed into the box.

I must say the early arrivals took it well. They'd already realised that judo is more than a sport. As an Oriental philosophy it encompasses aspects of the paranormal; and this disappearance of a stranger into a gymnastic box was clearly a manifestation of some unspoken mystery. It reflected well on their disciplined training that not a word of explanation was called for or given.

After a fruitless vigil throughout the two hour session – not a blink from the light – I returned to my room deflated. Almost immediately a white faced pupil knocked and entered.

"I've just had twelve pounds pinched from my pocket," he stammered.

I led him quickly into the changing room. In a loud, clear voice, which must have puzzled those who weren't privy to the trap, I said:

"Show me exactly where the money was taken from."

He pointed at a coat hook, but there was no response from the box. The silence was ominous.

"Show me exactly . . ." I repeated more loudly.

The top of the box shot up.

"The moment has come for me to disclose my presence." Chivers must have rehearsed the phrase in the box, and he delivered it with as much dignity as can be mustered by a man in a wooden horse. The entire group, in various states of undress, remained motionless. Their eyes were on Chivers whose dramatic appearance was a bewildering surprise to most of them. Disquiet aroused by changing rooms was clearly confirmed.

"What did you see Inspector?" I was Dr Watson again.

"Not a thing."

At that moment, my previously suppressed doubts resurfaced. Did Chivers possess sufficient sagacity for this assignment?

"Never mind," he said, sensing my disappointment. "We'll catch him next week." It sounded like a "Dick Barton" serial.

"I may not be able to get the cable next week – or the cushions!" My vindictive petulance was quite unnecessary.

It was with a faint heart that I packed him into the box the following Thursday. The class now accepted this routine as an integral part of the evening programme. However I had underrated Inspector Chivers' knowledge of the criminal mind, and was all the more astonished when he burst into the class at the conclusion of the warming-up exercises.

"Carry on breathing," I commanded as I turned to him.

Chivers' self control had again deserted him, and my first thought was that the bicycle accident was having a recurring effect.

"He's escaped!"

Class discipline broke down, and they crowded round.

"There were two left changing," explained the Inspector. "When the other one joined the class he thought he was alone, and started going through the pockets. I sprang up, but became lodged in the box." His trousers, I saw, had suffered further damage. "He was out like a shot, and I chased him round the building. But he got away! What are they going to say at the station? I'll lose my job. What am I going to do?"

Confinement in the box had obviously deranged Sherlock Holmes' judgment, so Dr Watson took charge of the situation:

"Who was in the changing room last? You, Thompson? Well, who was in there with you? Oh. you don't know his name, but you've seen him in the Bishopston area – then he's probably a resident. Pass me the class register. Mmm – three Bishopston addresses. Answer your names. Only two here from Bishopston. There's your man Chivers!"

"How did you deduce that?" He didn't actually call me Holmes.

"Never mind that now. Just get on your bike, and go get him."

"But my wheel's buckled." It was pitiful.

53

"Then you'll have to ride pillion," said my enterprising assistant who owned a scooter.

Chivers got his man – a young man as it turned out – and the young man's mother extracted a confession from him. When he appeared in court some months later he was commended by the judge for his initiative in trying to get to sea. However he was advised not to use other people's money in future.

Chivers finally became Bristol's Chief Constable. My assistant went into a monastery, and his successor constructed a trebuchet in his back garden. Two of the class became international competitors and won numerous medals. One became a Councillor, and another built a judo club in a cow shed. An older member took up Pelmanism and Scientology, and a thin boy tried the Spanish guitar.

A pensioner continued to attend regularly at a reduced fee for the sake of the showers; he later turned to high diving. The rest eventually gave up changing rooms.

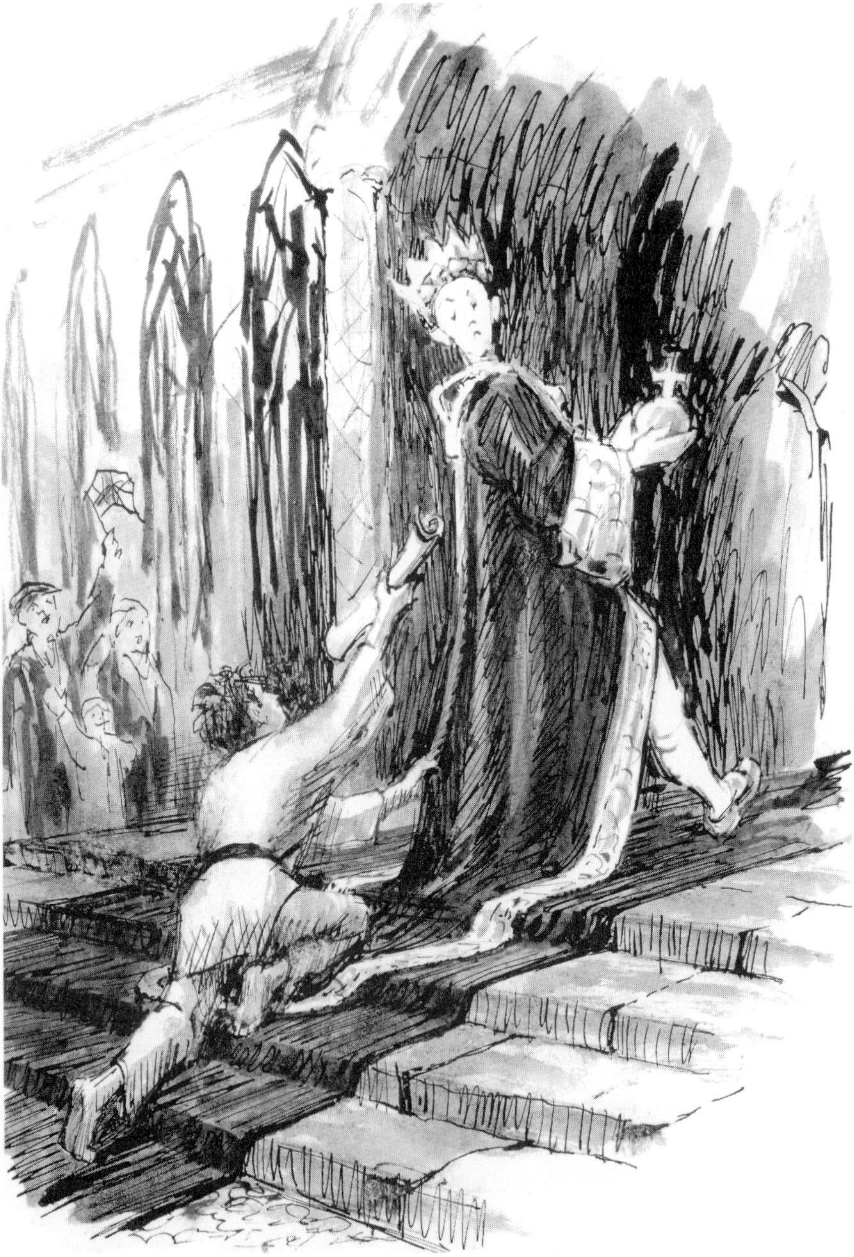

Feline Privilege

"A cat may look at a king," said Alice. "I've read that in some book, but I don't remember where."

The Duke of Edinburgh was a sad disappointment to Judokwai Bristol. However it must be said in mitigation that his reply to my letter was not written by him personally. The most significant statement it contained read:

"You could hardly expect His Royal Highness to take action in a matter of local rates."

It was clear that His Royal Highness had not been given the opportunity to consider why I most certainly did expect him to take action and use his influence with the Queen. A crie de coeur had been deliberately concealed from his attention lest the pettifogging tyrannies of Local Government should be majestically overruled by the Royal Prerogative. That was my reading of the palatial communication!

I had not resorted to the monarchy lightly; but the simple justice of our case had eluded the stereotyped thinking which stifles local administration. My appeal was not for personal relief, but for the survival of Judokwai Bristol.

Since my introduction of judo to Cotham Grammar School in 1951 the spread of "the gentle art" had been remarkable. A proliferation of school clubs and evening classes had brought unique educational benefits to hundreds of Bristolians; and evangelical work was proceeding throughout the country. This cultural crusade owed an inestimable debt to the club entitled "Judokwai Bristol."

Such had been the gist of my introduction to the letter of supplication submitted to the Duke of Edinburgh. (Similar entreaties had been sent to the Duchess of Albermarle, the Archbishop of Canterbury and the Prime Minister.) There had followed a short rhetorical passage:

> Where are Bristol's teachers and coaches trained? Where do I train myself? Where do the most dedicated practitioners in the West train for two hours before breakfast in the depths of winter? Who attracts the distinguished visiting sensei from London and Japan? Where do Bristol's school children enhance their metaphysical status and enter examinations? Where is the vibrant nucleus of this astonishing voluntary programme which so splendidly

fulfils the stated aspirations of the nation's leaders? (And here I had quoted chapter and verse from the report of the Duchess and public statements by the other recipients of my letter) – The irrefutable answer to all these questions (I had triumphantly declared) is – JUDOKWAI BRISTOL.

I had then acquainted His Royal Highness as persuasively as possible with the precise origin and nature of our dilemma:

A non profit making, educational and sporting organisation – very limited resources – meagre mats on which to practice – transported from pillar to post – years of fruitless search for a permanent home – temporary refuge in church halls, pavilions and disused warehouses – nowhere able to offer exclusive use – mats laid and raised at every session – resultant deformity of the surface directly responsible for sprains, displaced cartilages, subluxation of the vertebra and stubbed toes – reduction of carnage by stretching a canvas cover from screw eyes inserted into wooden floors – threats of eviction by landlord incensed at holes left by screw eyes (I omitted to mention that I had personally witnessed Wolf Cubs in Goodhind Street Church Hall provoke Arkela to incoherent rage by pushing his pencils through the screw holes. Details like this can add a ring of authenticity; but I judged that if my letter exceed six pages it might lose the bite of brevity).

We had eventually invested our savings in the purchase of a surplus R.A.F. wooden hut which the club members, under the direction of Charlie Gardner, had dismantled and stacked in a corner of Robinson's Removals yard. Sooner or later Robinson's were bound to find out. (This aspect had been phrased "economically" in order to demonstrate to His Royal Highness our enterprise and resourcefulness without suggesting irresponsible disregard for lawful procedures.)

Bristol Education Committee had been approached for a possible site on which to erect our hut. After protracted correspondence in which we had rehearsed the arguments already outlined they granted us, in lieu of a piece of land, sole use of a prefabricated building in a remote corner of an outlying school. We installed the wooden floor of our hut under the mats for improved shock absorbency and celebrated the first session not concluded by returning the mats to storage. They were to remain in place until the next session. We had a home of our own. It seemed that our problems were finally resolved – until we received the rates bill! On top of rent the sum demanded was far beyond our resources. It exceeded our annual income.

This was the tragic position in which we now found ourselves, I had explained to His Royal Highness (with the utmost brevity); and I had enclosed a copy of the rates bill, all relevant correspondence and the club's most recent balance sheet.

I had assured our treasurer, Reg Lomax, "We are a charitable organisation eligible for rate relief." It was a naive assumption made in ignorance of the infinite labyrinths of prevarication down which civil servants retreat before unaccustomed requests. I had summarised, for His Royal Highness, the circuitous correspondence which had followed by stating quite simply that our request for rate relief had been refused and that even Bristol's Lord Mayor had felt powerless to intervene. Brevity had remained uppermost in my mind.

These were the events, I had concluded with respectful humility towards His Royal Highness, that compelled me to seek intervention from national leaders who had expressed concern for the spiritual and physical well being of the country. The fate of our club and all it represented rested in His Hands.

Having thus laid out our case so clearly and concisely it was, as I said, a grave disappointment that first the Duke of Edinburgh closely followed by the Duchess and Archbishop all failed to meet the challenge posed by the plight of Judokwai Bristol. Our faith in the Great and the Good was profoundly shaken, and it was with diminished optimism that I awaited the response of the Prime Minister.

It is to the eternal credit of Harold MacMillan that he alone finally grasped the full implications of my appeal. His first reply contained little more than sympathetic suggestions about seeking legal advice; but I responded in more fulsome detail, explaining the precarious financial structure of the club. I surmised that with his wide experience as Chancellor of the Exchequer he would recognise the practical impossibility of his well intentioned advice. He did. And it was then that he demonstrated his unique sagacity . . .

In a further carefully worded reply he said unequivocally that the solution to our problem seemed to lie with the Chief Education Officer; and with remarkable grasp of detail the Prime Minister named him personally!

Mr G.H. Sylvester summoned me immediately to the Council House on receipt of my letter. He knew me well as a correspondent; but we had not met personally since my appointment as a Bristol teacher. The letter from Downing Street, which I had enclosed, was in his hand as I entered. No doubt he was flattered by the PM's trust in his personal ability to deal with an extraordinary crisis.

"Well, Mr Hicks. it certainly looks as though we shall have to do something for you." He smiled conspiratorially and for the first time in this long campaign I scented victory. A wink seemed too presumptuous, so I responded with a deferential lift if the eyebrows. In answer to some probing questions I affirmed that I was not a transitory petitioner. I was in Bristol to stay. This was intended to assure him of my continuing commitment, but he betrayed no visible relief. What I did obtain was the assurance of G.H. Sylvester that henceforth the Education Committee would meet our rates bill in full. This remarkable concession, made shortly before his retirement, was to ensure his place in the history of Judokwai Bristol.

Members of the Western Judo Association were quietly impressed by these negotiations with exalted persons, and none more so than the chairman – "Spud" Murphy. He had a striking resemblance to the TV detective Frank Cannon, a natural flair for organisation and a deep seated belief in the persuasive powers of belligerence. The story of our success soon reached his club's waterlogged shack. The members had to break up patches of ice on their mats before practice, so he had a conditioned empathy with our predicament.

Whilst Spud never flinched from confrontation with the British Judo Association's officers, whom he regarded with great disdain, he had never confronted our political, religious or Royal leaders. My successful enlistment of the PM as a patron of judo dispelled his initial scepticism about our chances of success and made a deep impression on him. Thence forth, in moments of crisis, he would say:

"Better get Jerry Hicks to write to the Prime Minister."

In retrospect I realise that this policy of last resort was to have far, far wider consequences than either of us anticipated but that's another story . . .

Some years later, as a founder member of the South West Sports Council, I attended the first meeting in Taunton's salubrious County Hall; and the problem of tax relief for sports clubs aroused an earnest debate – which has continued unresolved for 25 years.

I gathered my courage and signalled to Mr Morrison, the MP sitting in the chair, that I wished to speak. He acceded.

"The best way of dealing with this problem, in my experience, is to write to the Prime Minister." My words brought gasps and grunts of indignation from the scores of Local Councillors assembled. They were rather contemptuous of the three naive representatives of sport.

"Rates have nothing to do with National Government," was the immediate crushing response.

However I still feel glad that Mr MacMillan and I were unaware of this distinction: and I also remain tetchy that the likes of Sir Humphrey Appleby denied Judokwai Bristol the Royal Prerogative of Mercy and ecclesiastical absolution from the burden of local rates.

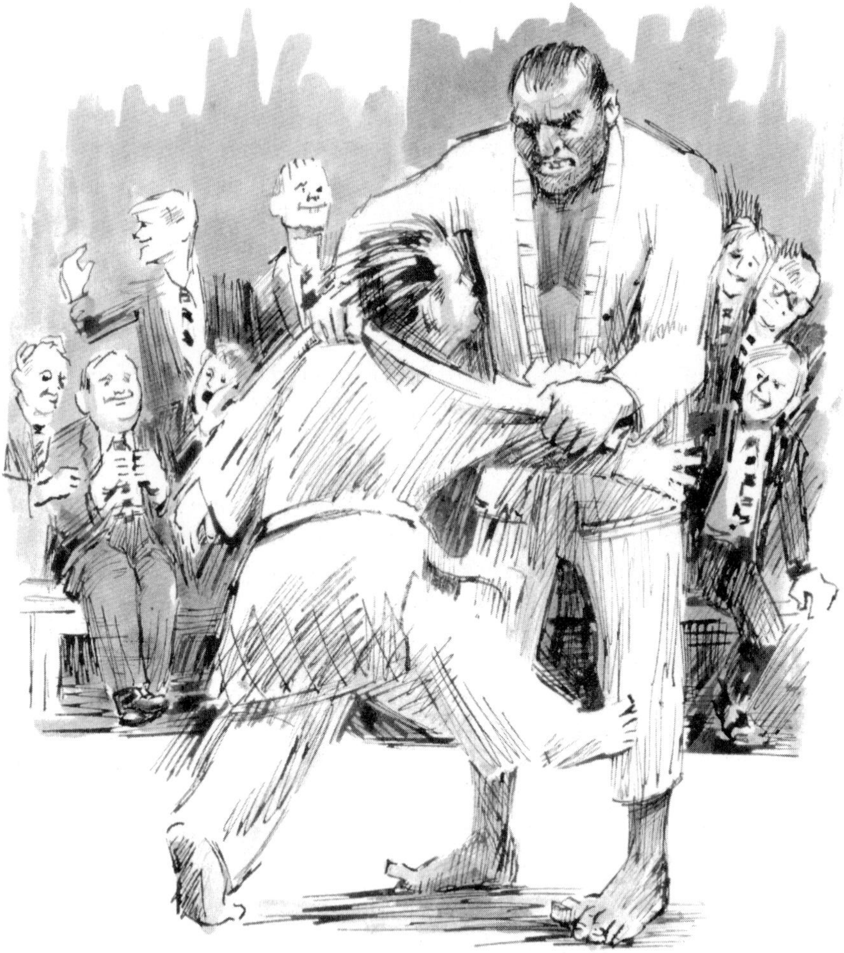

Special Powers

In a minute or two the Caterpillar took the hookah out of its mouth and yawned once or twice, and shook itself. Then it got down off the mushroom and crawled away into the grass merely remarking as it went, "One side will make you grow taller and the other side will make you grow shorter."

"Excuse me, Mr Hicks. Would it be all right for me to join the school judo club? I haven't done any before, but I thought it might be a good idea to have a go." The blink behind his glasses had a certain earnest appeal.

I hope that I concealed my surprise at this unexpected request from our new Maths teacher Philip Rudkin. (I have disguised his identity behind this alias for reasons that will become apparent.) Cotham Grammar School boys constantly asked me at most unlikely moments if there were any vacancies in the club, but it had been a long time since a member of staff had ventured to join the fray. They were far too concerned about the propriety of entering into physical combat with the young ruffians whom the headmaster optimistically addressed as "Gentlemen".

Also I must confess that Rudkin seemed to me a particularly unlikely candidate for the rough and tumble of a judo club – however well ordered the procedures. Short and plump with an air of bespectacled diffidence, he was known in the staff room to be having discipline problems with unruly elements in the fourth year. It later emerged that he was an outstanding swimmer; but his athleticism was not apparent in his general demeanour which marked him down as another potential victim.

However, with only a moment's hesitation, I replied as encouragingly as I could manage:

"Yes, of course, I'd be glad of some help. I run two lunch hour sessions a week on Monday and Wednesday. Come and join us as soon as you've got some kit – or judo-gi as we call it!" Oriental terminology had a reassuring ring of authenticity.

I trotted out further details before we were summoned to our classes in Pavlovian style by the next bell.

It crossed my mind that Rudkin had probably been directed to the judo club by the headmaster. Sammy would have certainly been aware of Rudkin's difficulties, and he shrewdly suspected that the

Spartan discipline I had established in the Art Room was a product of my martial sport. Perhaps he felt that a little Samurai rigour would strengthen Rudkin's powers of command.

Cotham enjoyed a national reputation for its prowess in traditional team sports, and I had been rather diffident about introducing a modest alternative, especially as, in response to some discreet enquiries, my colleagues assured me that Sammy was far too conservative to tolerate anything as alien as judo. He readily admitted that his first inclination was to refuse all requests.

So I had begun, rather deviously, by teaching a little judo to a couple of intrepid teachers after school. The banging had attracted Sammy's curiosity on more than one occasion and our esoteric activity clearly fascinated him. Eventually he drew me to one side and said:

"When are you going to teach this to the boys?"

"I shall need a canvas cover for the mats," I replied instantly; and then added as irresistible inducement, "A matter of safety."

Seeing no sign of refusal and emboldened by the favourable tide I pressed my advantage.

"And I'll need a dozen judo suits – at least!"

One of the earliest Dual Use deals was made with an Evening Institute for whom I agreed (not without some misgiving) to use the same equipment for an adult class at Cotham. Thus Britain's first officially recognised school judo club was launched – exactly ten years after my illicit enterprise as a schoolboy.

Sammy was very proud of his initiative. Club sessions were inundated with visiting inspectors, local politicians and P.E. advisers. Our pioneering enterprise was soon required for demonstrations at national conferences where judo was recommended as fervently as the trampoline and circuit training. Even visitors to the Art Room were informed by Sammy:

"Mr Hicks is also a Judo Expert," and invariably the excruciatingly witty reply was:

"Well I shouldn't like to meet him on a dark night." I refrained from asking if they lived in fear of fencers challenging them to duels or archers placing apples on their heads.

Such misplaced adulation was particularly embarrassing whilst I was working my way up through the Kyu grades who wear coloured belts. When, after four years, I became the first living black belt in the west country Sammy was full of congratulations though he treated the award as belated recognition of "my special powers".

"You must never let the boys provoke you into acts of physical chastisement. The Courts would take a very serious view because of 'your special powers'. Join a Union with a good legal service just in case."

Serious provocation rarely occurred since the boys were as much in awe of "my special powers" as was Sammy. When an unusually truculent fifth former tried to escape from a detention I cut off his retreat to the door by vaulting over a table, and his mates, who were watching through the window, shouted:

"Watch out Greg, or he'll judo you!" Perhaps Sammy was not so far wrong in his perception of the criminal mind . . .

Initially the club did a lot of breakfall practice, as was the custom in those days: and the reverberations in the dining room below the gym sounded like a sustained thunder storm. Sammy dismissed staff complaints as frivolous. Once the real fighting started it was not long before senior boys could throw adults on their back with considerable relish. Recruitment of teachers ceased.

It was, therefore, with caution bred from experience that I introduced Rudkin to the club. On his first appearance in a new judo suit which was several sizes too big and worn with the knot of the belt above the navel, the hard lads eyed him like cannibals calculating the cooking time for a particularly succulent missionary. It required my constant ingenuity to keep the new assistant out of harm's way for a week or two. When the boys finally got their hands on him, I noted, with some relief, that Rudkin displayed a defiant stability which was harder to dislodge than they had expected. Nevertheless he suffered some rather heavy falls, and I wondered how long his body and dignity would survive.

Yet Rudkin was not discouraged and persevered with quiet determination. He began to develop a surprisingly powerful Tsurikomi-goshi – a hip throw well suited to his low centre of gravity. Even the most skilful boys started to treat his attacks with respect.

Unfortunately he was very susceptible to being held on the ground, so I concentrated my coaching on improving this aspect of his armoury.

"You've no need to tap submission immediately I secure a holding. It may be uncomfortable, but that's no reason to give up. You only submit to avoid serious injury or death from arm locks and strangles. In a competition you have 30 seconds in which to escape from a holding. Don't tap until the referee calls 'Ippon'. That means its all over – the equivalent of a knock out."

Rudkin dutifully flayed about like an up-turned turtle until I released him. His fighting spirit was not entirely dormant.

At the end of his first term I was able to announce to the club:

"In two weeks time I shall be examining at an outside 'grading'. This will be an excellent opportunity for you to compete for your next coloured belt: but don't expect any favours – you'll have to earn it. Give your names to Mr Rudkin. He will, in fact, be entering himself."

On the appointed Saturday morning I was surprised to find that the church hall, where Judokwai Bristol were holding the "grading", was packed with spectators. Closer inspection revealed that they were largely composed of Cotham Grammar School supporters.

"Is Mr Rudkin going to have a go then, Sir?"

"Yes, that's right." I tried to sound detached.

Rudkin was already changed, and seated on his own next to the piano. He resembled a church organist who was obliging with his services at a Buddhist ceremony dressed in ritual clothing borrowed from some gigantic monk.

In those days competitors were matched by grade regardless of weight. The only constraint was that one tried to avoid matching players from the same club. Some of our boys were amongst the early competitors, and they disposed of adult opposition with considerable confidence. Their supporters were enthusiastic: but I sensed that the main attraction was still to come.

Their attention was fully engaged when Rudkin's name was finally called. His opponent emerged as a member of the National Dock Labour Board Judo Club. They were known as a hard bunch, and their instructor often recounted the comments of one docker who fell 20 feet from a crane onto concrete.

"But I was OK" he said. "I remembered me breakfall – the old one two."

Rudkin's opponent looked hard even by NDLB standards. He was a gigantic man with a slight stoop and long hairy arms that protruded from a shrunken jacket and terminated almost at his knees. As this Goliath stepped onto the mats the delighted expectancy amongst Cotham's followers was more suited to a pack of jackals than to the children of Israel.

Rudkin carefully removed his spectacles, placed them on the piano, strode forward and bowed with calm resolution. The referee shouted "Hajime". Rudkin took hold of Goliath about waist height, and the giant reached down to seize his opponent's collar.

It may have been that the dockers practised in very restricted circumstances, or perhaps that Goliath saw no special merit in unnecessary movement. Whatever the reason, he planted his two huge feet firmly in the centre of the mat area, and, having established his territory, declined to budge.

Rudkin, on the other hand, was accustomed to a certain amount of preliminary jigging about; so he made every effort to coax his adversary into action. But, suspended on the end of Goliath's grappling arm by the collar, his gyrations in a small semi-circle around two monumental stationary legs resembled the erratic actions of a badly handled marionette. He made a couple of tentative foot sweeps but Goliath only winced. I was uneasy lest any more reckless kicking should arouse the giant's anger.

Rudkin also must have realised the necessity for a change of tactics. With courageous determination he swivelled at the waist, turning his back on Goliath. The intention was Tsuri-komi goshi, and for one incredible moment, as the veins swelled on Rudkin's head, I thought he might succeed. To have brought the giant crashing over his head would have been spectacular, and the audience gasped in anticipation. Our club members looked anxiously at the piano which had only recently been repaired.

Had Goliath remained rigid he might well have been thrown; but, sensing his absurd danger, he buckled his knees – and for an instant Rudkin supported a total of about 30 stone! It was too much. He collapsed under the strain, and a mountain of muscle subsided on top of him.

Goliath had only to embrace Rudkin's head with his grappling arm and a hold crudely akin to Kesa-gatame was secured. The referee shouted "Osae-komi", the timekeeper checked his watch and a docker in the audience, who could not contain his excitement, shouted "Squeeze!"

Although, in that archaic period of British judo, audience participation was considered ill-mannered and disruptive, I overlooked this breach of etiquette lest I should appear biased; but I felt far from detached. Disaster seemed imminent!

Goliath was not content with maintaining his hold for 30 seconds. He appeared to have formed a fervent dislike for the shape of Rudkin's head. By digging his heels into the mats and joining his hands he made strenuous efforts to crush the offending cranium against his chest – occasionally pausing for breath and a quick glance to see how the reshaping was progressing.

Rudkin barely twitched and I wondered if he would remain conscious for 30 seconds. Escape was not even a consideration. The Cotham boys could scarce conceal their glee, and they cast covert glances in my direction. Even if Rudkin should prove fit for school on Monday morning I could imagine the derisive questions. By Friday the word would have spread and even the first year would be asking him slyly:

"Have you got your black belt yet, Sir?"

And then the impossible happened. Just as the timekeeper was about to signal the expiration of 30 seconds and the referee was bracing himself for the expiration of Rudkin, Goliath let out a mighty roar of pain and tapped submission. The referee had no option but to call "Ippon".

The audience were incredulous. Goliath lurched to his feet and bowed clumsily as the referee raised his arm towards the victorious Rudkin. The humiliated giant stumbled out and was unavailable for further contests. Rudkin betrayed no surprise. He made a solemn bow, returned to the piano, resumed his seat and replaced his spectacles. His expression was one of inscrutable detachment.

"What happened then, Sir?" a boy whispered in my ear.

"What did he do to 'im?" And similar unanswered questions were repeated in awed undertones.

The Cotham boys' confusion was understandable. Had Rudkin been made privy to "special powers" – some secret pressure point known only to holders of the coveted black belt? I repelled all questions with a knowing shake of the head; but secretly I was as curious as they were.

Rudkin was called for two more contests, and it is difficult to say whether the results were due to inspiration gained from his extraordinary victory over Goliath; or whether his opponents, who had witnessed an apparent miracle, were paralysed with fear. He certainly scored with two superb Tsuri-komi-goshi throws, and I had no hesitation in promoting him two grades.

From that day Rudkin's discipline problems were resolved. By the time the legend reached the first year every embellishment had been embellished. His entries into classrooms were marked by the speed with which the young gentlemen sprang silently to their feet in respect for the occult. As we stalked side by side through the playgrounds on our duty roster I no longer had any need to shout:

"Pick up that litter, child."

A bespectacled enigmatic glance from the Sheriff's Deputy and an imperious wave of his hand was enough to compel the most belligerent minions to scurry into action like a swarm of Prime Ministers gathering litter for the TV cameras.

The following year Philip was promoted to a senior post in a northern school and we never met again. A legendary law-man rode off into the sunset.

It was some months after the historic grading competition before I met Goliath at a judo club. My curiosity could no longer be contained.

"By the way," I said in an off-hand manner, "what made you submit at your last grading when you were in such a strong position?"

He gave a wry shake of his bowed head.

"That little bloke I was on with. Never known a head like it! Talk about hard! I squeezed it so tight I broke two of me own ribs."

I thought at the time it was best not to mention this revelation to Rudkin; and to have told the boys would have been an act of gross betrayal.

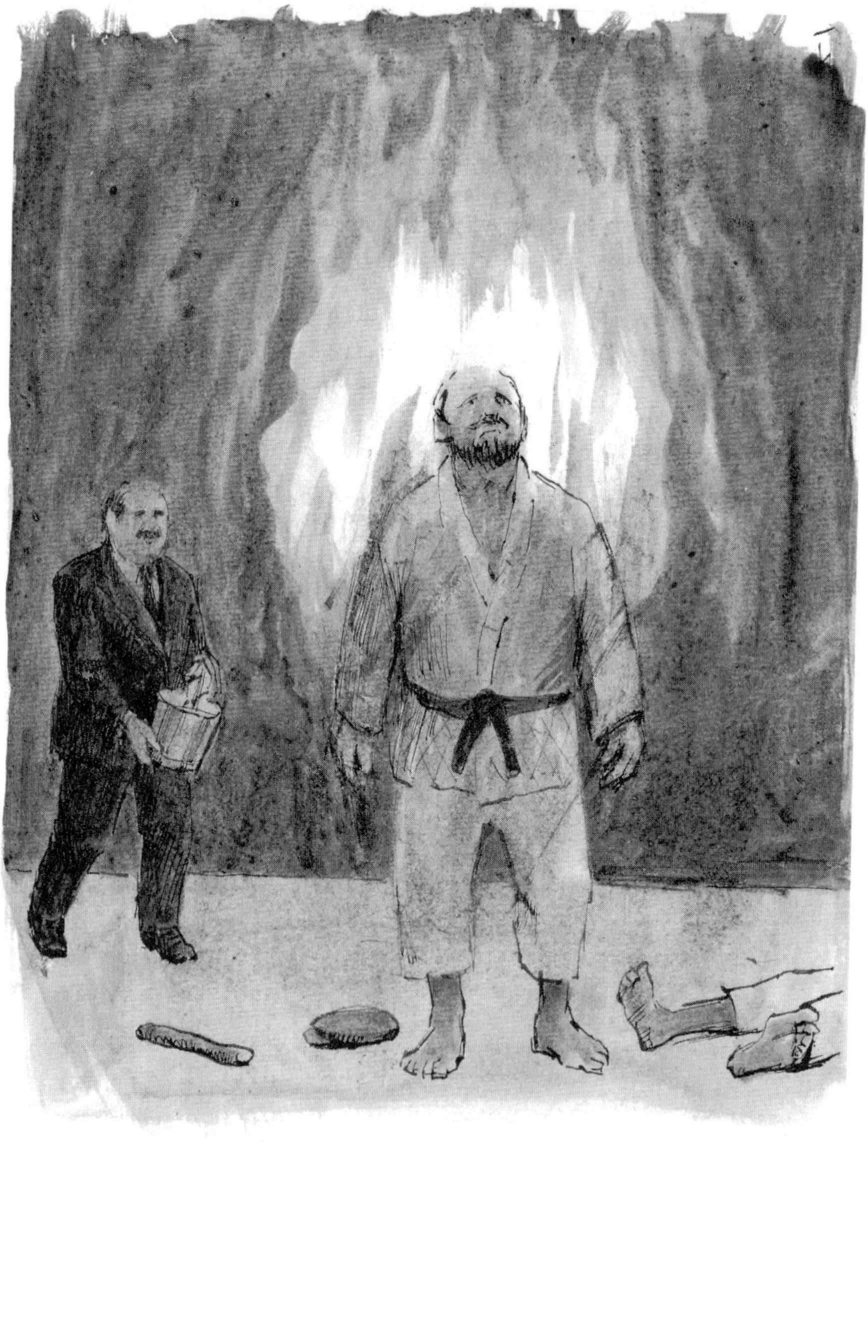

The Spanner

"You know," he added very gravely, "it's one of the most serious things that can possibly happen to one in a battle – to get one's head cut off."

The first time I saw a self defence demonstration go wrong was during a judo display in the Town Hall at Taunton. As the west country's first living black belt, I was a guest performer together with an ageing London 2nd dan whose fighting days were a wistful memory. There seemed to be no tactful way of expressing my misgivings about our roles; but, in any case, no one could have anticipated the debacle that was to follow.

A glance at the programme confirmed that the well tried Music Hall formula was being strictly adhered to. It was "on the boards" of these wooden stages in 1889 that Yukio Tani had introduced ju-jitsu or Bartitsu, as this forerunner of judo was variously called, to an astonished public. Even though Hackenschmidt and Sandow refused Tani's challenges, his remarkable skill against all comers earned him "star billing" on the Halls.

Such is the force of habit that 50 years later the Albert Hall still presented judo shows with a Palace of Varieties format; and Taunton produced a provincial imitation.

An opening "mass randori" was a curious equivalent of an opening chorus of Gaiety Girls. Whereas the girls in frilly petticoats squeaked and kicked their legs, pairs of judo men in white pyjamas grunted and kicked each other. The Taunton grunts were a pale imitation of the Samurai's "kiai" scream "emanating from the lower abdomen" – with which Shaw Desmond claimed to have felled an Oxford graduate at 20 paces. However they arrested the attention of a rural audience and induced a receptive frame of mind for the variety acts to follow.

The Albert Hall invariably boasted aged "sensei" who demonstrated ritual "katas". They glided as in a trance wearing imaginary armour, and the commentator's Japanese terminology deepened the mystification. The Taunton kata was less refined, but the audience no less mystified.

When the 2nd dan and I were introduced as the star performers I felt very inadequate; and my discomfort was not eased when my partner stubbed out a cigarette and whispered:

"One throw for you and two for me – OK?" As a first dan I could hardly object.

After our painfully contrived "randori", which convinced only the uninitiated, we were really fighting, my panting colleague was invited to fell ten men as the climax before the interval. The Music Halls traditionally reserved this prestigious slot for Grimaldi, Dan Leno or some other star comedian. It was an ominous precedent.

A young champion could usually dispatch ten consecutive opponents in under five minutes – even if some misguided fellow sought to throw a spanner in the works by "digging in" defensively, "Trying to make a name for himself," the respectful would mutter contemptuously. As the tenth man was triumphantly buried with a spectacular throw, the reverential silence, which then prevailed at all judo events, would give way to appreciative applause.

These displays of fighting skill differed subtly from grading exams, held within the judo fraternity, when all competitive dan grades were required to defeat a line of opponents. When appearing in public, holders of "the coveted black belt" were expected to perform effortlessly; so unspoken rules were observed. The selected ten were not told to "jump" for the star performer in so many words; but perverse attempts to threaten the desired outcome were despised. Usually this unwritten code prevailed. Taunton was an exception.

The first seven were thrown with the style which never quite deserts a man who has been good in his day. His wheezing was barely perceptible; and a triumphant conclusion seemed assured – when he discovered too late that number eight was "a spanner".

This wretched brown belt seized an unexpected chance of glory when the fading star stumbled to the ground from sheer fatigue. In a flash the Spanner dived on his victim whose breath escaped with an audible hiss. As the referee, I could have called them to their feet had they been near the edge of the platform – but they were bang in the middle. The hold was secure. I had only one option:

Holding out my arm, as a signal to the time keeper, I called as impassively as I could manage, "Holding!"

The show was crumbling around me. For the star to tap submission was unthinkable; but the prolonged ignominy of being held down for the required 30 seconds was worse. The Music Halls had also known disaster – as when three circus acrobats formed "a span of life" across a ravine to enable the heroine to escape the lecherous strong man by running over their backs. Alas! On the opening night, as the human bridge fell into place, the top man missed his grip on the far side and the deception of supporting invisible wires was exposed. Before a frantic stage manager brought down the curtain, the three acrobats were seen floating in space!

There was no curtain to conceal my embarrassment at Taunton. I stood like a ring master watching a lion eat its tamer.

Then, as I bent over the entwined catastrophe, looking vainly for some technical excuse to retrieve the situation, I heard the exhausted black belt whisper:

"Get up."

The Spanner failed, or chose not, to comprehend. He tightened his grip.

"Get up!" repeated his victim, manfully summoning up an authority which had not entirely deserted a dying king.

Robbed and incredulous, the Spanner rose with a growing realisation that he'd boobed. He dutifully fell to the next attack and the next two conscripts had enough perception to do likewise. A naive audience presumed that some obscure technicality had intruded into a display of invincible skill.

At the sausage roll reception in the interval the Lord Mayor complimented the star:

"You must be incredibly fit and skillful to beat ten men in quick succession." The star gave a modest, self deprecating shrug. (Shortly afterwards he emigrated to Australia.)

It was with some relief that I took a seat in the audience for the second half – confident that nothing worse could happen. I was wrong.

The Taunton organisers had not forgotten the Music Hall speciality number; and judo's speciality was self defence.

A garbled version of these Samurai skills had become the province of an eccentric minority. They relished the drama of demonstrating Mr Motto's shield against all weapons of the ungodly (Bruce Lee had yet to appear). Imparting these secrets to rotund business men threatened by bookies brought modest financial rewards; but competitive judo men scorned these deceptions, and self defence was rarely, if ever, practised in orthodox judo clubs.

However, with the advent of a public display, a self defence addict always emerged with some bizarre speciality. His harmless deception presented initially a poker faced expert frustrating, from a seated position, attempts at assassination by the dreaded Ninja. This set his skills in an historical setting and confirmed public anxiety about Tongs, Triads and proprietors of Chinese restaurants.

Our hero then confronted a contemporary ruffian distinguished by the addition to his judo clothing of a cloth cap and muffler. The plausibility of the scenario did not bear rational examination. Cloth

Cap's choice of a man standing by a bus stop dressed in judo clothing for his initial abuse was improbable. After being dropped on his head for an attempted punch on the nose, his futile persistence with cudgel and knife was incredible. Nevertheless, the audience suspended their disbelief for the joy of seeing Cloth Cap dropped on his head again and again and again.

The climax of this fantasy was invariably a hold up from the rear with a loaded revolver – which no one believed for a moment. As our hero simultaneously spun round, parried and threw with a devastating o-soto-gari a deafening report from a blank cartridge would bring a gasp from the audience – followed by enthusiastic applause. During this acclamation Cloth Cap would remove his disguise – revealing himself as just another judo man. Sport and Variety became totally merged.

Imagine my horror at Taunton when I saw that the hero preparing to deal with Ninja and Cloth Cap was the disastrous Spanner! I watched the historical rituals with a miserable sense of foreboding. Ninja went down quite smoothly; the audience clapped; and my nervousness subsided.

Excitement mounted with the donning of cap and muffler. Shrewd suspicions as to who was the bad guy were fully confirmed, and anticipation of his punishment drew some ill mannered mirth from the Somerset yokels. It was, perhaps, their laughter which caused a lapse in concentration; but seldom can a self defence display have culminated in such a grotesque mistake.

The Spanner felt the gun in his back and spun to disarm – but either the parry was a fraction too late or the trigger finger a fraction too itchy. No one realised immediately. The gun exploded and the throw worked well. The Spanner, flushed with pride and effort acknowledged his acclaim and then turned to leave the platform . . .

It was not until he reached the changing room that he realised why his departure had aroused such howls of laughter. When he removed his jacket he discovered that the blank cartridge had left a large black mark plumb in the middle of his back!

I was in such a hurry to depart that I left behind my Army Surplus beaver hat.

Some months later Judokwai Bristol organised the Western Area Display at the Colston Hall (though famous for its music, it is not a Music Hall!). To my astonishment the Spanner and Cloth Cap offered to fill the obligatory self defence slot. Unfortunately the alternative was our own self defence addict – an elderly Welsh wizard who preferred to plant his stooge in the audience. "What the public want is drama." he once confided in me. Reg reported that, at a recent fête, our hero's deception was exposed and he had only been saved from some irate youths by the intervention of Peter Stowell, a professional bouncer. So with heavy hearts the Spanner was accepted.

I gently reminded him of Taunton and pressed him to remove the blank cartridges. It was to no avail. The Spanner was adamant:

"Don't worry," he announced with sublime self confidence. "There'll be no mistake this time!"

I captained my own club to victory in the team match and for the fifth year in succession we were awarded the Bob Taylor Shield. This was named after a gallant young judo player, mentioned earlier, who was shot dead when attempting to apprehend two bank robbers. They were hanged and he was posthumously awarded the first black belt in the west country. It was a bitter irony that, although this real life tragedy had failed to convince the self defence addicts of the danger in confronting gunmen, the Spanner's grotesque climax was a more effective warning. It was certainly the last self defence act in our association for over thirty years.

Once again the Spanner felt the gun in his back, spun and parried too late. I watched in horror as if seeing a slow motion re-run. This time he did not have to wait until he reached the changing room before he knew he was "dead".

As he turned to acknowledge his applause the back of his jacket burst into flames. The picturesque effect brought loud cheers from the audience; but the Spanner seemed unaware of his spontaneous combustion. He stood motionless like some pantomime demon – quite literally in a blaze of glory. Unfortunately escape down a Music Hall trap door was denied him.

In that prolonged moment of fascination and disbelief our regional chairman demonstrated his remarkable presence of mind. Moving with the unexpected dexterity of Frank Cannon (his TV "look alike") he sprang onto the stage clutching a fire bucket full of water. With one splendid "sploosh" the Spanner was put out. It was a symbolic action.

Next day the press reported:

"Judo as a form of self defence was shown by a brown belt from Taunton although had the whole thing been in earnest one cannot but think the demonstrator would have been a dead man."

I was sorry that the Spanner left our association and joined the rival AJA who were said to be more generous with their dan grades. The Taunton police would never have traced my beaver hat and dispatched it to me by special patrol if he had not impressed on them the importance of someone entitled to wear "the coveted black belt". He continued to demonstrate self defence and I heard that on one occasion he performed at a cinema dressed as a gladiator. He was ahead of his time.

Peter, the bouncer, told me that he visited the Spanner in hospital shortly before his premature death – which was not caused by self defence.

"I tried to cheer him up," said Peter with unexpected tenderness. 'I said, "This is justice on you for joining the AJA'."

I'm glad he didn't mention the Colston Hall.

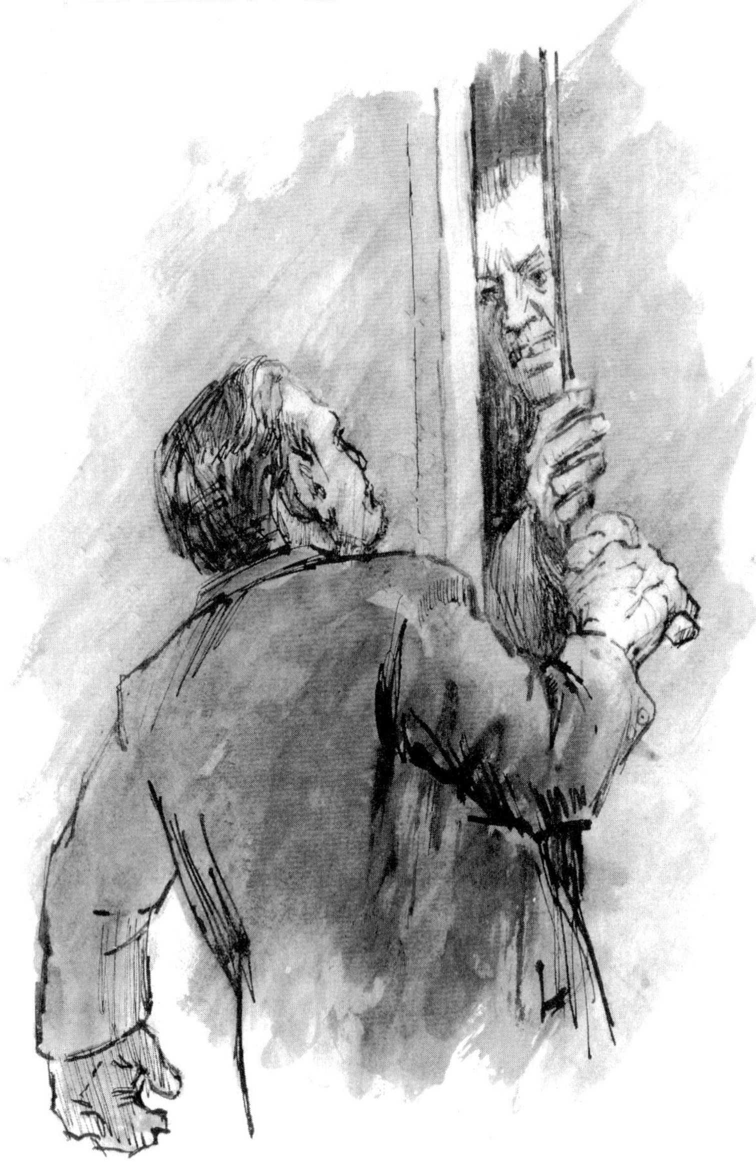

Davids and Goliaths

"And hast thou slain the Jabberwock?
Come to my arms my beamish boy!
O frabjous day! Callooh! Callay!"
He chortled in his joy.

A judo weekend at the Crystal "Chlorinated" Palace was over. Competition on Saturday had been followed by a National Grading on Sunday, which had been concluded less than an hour since. The west country contingent were driving home. "Westward, westward, always westward – to the setting of the sun."

Our convoy stopped at the first Indian restaurant in the Fulham Road. It may have been a Simla Indian restaurant, for the menu was not dissimilar from many others we had encountered. A lonely waiter responded eagerly to the unexpected influx, and arranged seating for about a dozen. Bert sat next to me.

"You seemed to be having a good day at the grading, Bert. How did you get on?"

"A few more points towards me black belt. But, Jerry! Did you see that gorilla they put me on with?"

Bert reminds me of Harry Secombe's self parody, "I was six feet tall – 'til a lift fell on me!" Hammered down to a little over five feet high, with a boxer's nose and a seaman's eye, "weather beaten" is an apt description. He came to judo late in life, after a career in the Navy; and with dogged determination set about the formidable task of earning a black belt.

"Did you beat him, Bert?"

"Lost on a penalty."

"What did you do? Step over the red line?"

"I know better than that, Jerry. No. But when I looked at the size of him, I thought there'd been a mistake. Don't they do these things in weight categories?"

"Not always at gradings. I usually try to match opponents for size, if I'm examining."

"Well they didn't! I looks over at the referee as much as to say, 'What about this, then?' But he just says. 'Come on, get on with it.' I should think this gorilla was about three times my size; but I wasn't going to be intimidated. So I bows and pushes me jacket back with both hands, like Geof Gleeson used to do.

"'Stop that!' he shouts, and points to the ground. I thought there must be a hole in the mats. 'Kneel down,' he says. 'What's all this about then?' I says; but I kneels down like he tells me. Then he points down at me and shouts, 'Keikoku!' Well I know what that means. It means you done something seriously wrong – something dangerous.

"'What have I done?' I says.

"'I saw what you done,' he says. 'You deliberately disarranged your judo clothing.'

"'Well, I ask you!' I just kneels there, and I looks up at this great gorilla, and I says, 'God forbid that I should take advantage of that man there.'

"'You watch it.' he says. 'You button your lip, or it'll be Hansokumake for you.'"

The waiter hovered around for our orders, and I passed the menu to Bert.

"After you." he said. So I ordered the ubiquitous chicken vindaloo, plain boiled rice, some dal, a poppadum and lime pickle.

"The same for me." said Bert.

Whilst the others were searching out the most scorching dishes on offer, I remembered Bert telling me of a barbaric flogging he received as a young seaman for thumping an officer. It didn't improve his respect for authority, and it occurred to me that the referee got off lightly.

"How's the job?" I inquired as an optimistic change of subject.

"Didn't I tell you? The Board Mills have closed down. I'm on the dole."

"That must be a new experience for you Bert."

"Never been off work in me life before. I had to go to the Labour Exchange. Someone said I could claim extra for the kids. So the next week this chap at the counter starts asking me all these questions. 'How many children have you got?' he says.

"Four." I says.

"What's the name of the eldest, and the date of birth?" he says.

"I gives him the name and says, 'He's fourteen, but I don't know his date of birth.'

"Don't know his date of birth!' and he gives me a look. 'Well, what's the name of the second?' he says. 'And his date of birth.'

"He was beginning to get up my nose, but I just says, 'She's a girl, and I don't know her date of birth either.'

"'Oh!' he says, and he gives me this look again. 'You don't know her date of birth either. I don't suppose you know the date of birth of the others, do you?' and he's getting right up my nose.

"'No, I don't.' I says.

"'You don't know much, do you?' and he looks at me as if I'm dirt.

"I would have hit him, but there's this glass screen between us . . ."

Our orders arrived, and Bert watched very carefully as I made a hole in the rice for the vindaloo. He did the same, and waited until I made a start before tasting his own. It was quite hot, but Bert did not seem to mind. Presently the pangs of hunger began to ease.

"What did you do about this bloke in the Labour Exchange?" I felt there was more to the story.

"Well, as I says, there's this sheet of glass between us; so I can't thump him. But there's a hole at the bottom where you push the forms through. And I sees his tie hanging down. So, quick as a flash, I reaches through and grabs it. He looks quite surprised, and starts to pull back. But I pulls and pulls 'til his face is right up against the glass, and his nose is as flat as mine. Then I says to him like this, I says:

"'I may not know much; but I know more than you think I do.'

"He can't say much with his face flat against the glass, but I can see he's pretty steamed up. So I starts looking to left and right to see which way he'll come through as soon as I lets go."

I was listening so intently that I failed to savour the last grain of rice, and felt quite impatient when the waiter asked if we wanted a sweet.

"Just some lychees." I said abruptly.

"Same for me." said Bert.

"What happened then, Bert?" I wondered if he had found a way of alighting from the tiger.

"I spots the door, and as I lets go we both run for it – and we gets there at the same time. He pulls the door open and tries to get through, and I pulls it shut – well as near shut as I can. Then he pulls it wider, and I pulls it back again."

He didn't have to elaborate. I could remember, all too vividly, trying to secure the door of a teacher's room with a rope round the handle when I was a schoolboy. He reached the door as I was fastening the other end to some bannisters, and we started this terrible tug-of-war. Eventually I had to make good the knot with the door slightly ajar; and he recognised me through the gap . . .

"What a predicament, Bert. And you hadn't even got a rope!"

"I knew I had to let go sooner or later. So I thought – well this is where me judo comes in. Now's the time to see if it works."

"Well, he came at me through the door like a cork out of a bottle. I threw him with me seoi-nage right over me shoulder; and he went like a bomb! Never worked better. I think he was winded, 'cos he just lay there. And an old woman comes up and says to him, 'Serve you right for picking on the little feller.'"

He paused as we savoured the cool firm texture of the lychees on our glowing palettes, and my mind turned to others who had put their judo to the test. Bob Taylor was shot before he could get to grips with escaping bank robbers. John Davies thought he'd won on the strength of his first two judo lessons. When an uncouth miscreant, who'd started a cafe brawl, subsequently confronted him with, "So you were the grass who called the police." and seized his jacket, John recognised this opening gambit and responded with an immaculate foot sweep. The miscreant went down with a bump; and John, having exhausted his repertoire, made the mistake of turning away. He received a severe blow on the back of his head from a bottle. The gash required six stitches.

Les, a rugged seasoned competitor, extended his vocabulary beyond judo techniques to avert retaliation. He rescued his mate from a gang beating, and felled about thirty assailants. A similar triumph against overwhelming odds by Horatius in Ancient Rome was rewarded with a monument and an epic poem. Les was sent to prison. Presumably his effective use of a pick axe handle, which left casualties lining the road, was regarded as excessive force.

However the most bizarre outcome of a judo response to intimidation must be that suffered by Jane Bridge. This pretty, red headed lightweight probably appeared very vulnerable as she cycled with her boyfriend back from their judo club. In fact she was Britain's first world champion. As I understand it, she responded to unwanted attentions from a car full of leather coated louts with a vulgar gesture. The two cyclists were then cornered by the car, when the first lout sprang out and advanced on Jane. She must have been desperate to attempt a throw against a man about eight stone heavier. But it worked! Then as the lout clumsily regained his feet he shouted, "What the hell do you think you're doing? We're the police!"

That's the story I heard, and the press report of the trial seemed to confirm it. The case brought against Jane for assaulting a police officer was laughed out of court. She could barely see over the dock! But she suffered months of miserable apprehension. A threatened judo player suffers double jeopardy. Lose, and he or she faces derision, injury or death. Win, and the prospect may be prison!

"Have you heard any more about it Bert?" I was still thinking of Jane Bridge.

"Well, sort of. I had to go in the next week with me kid's dates of birth. I was thinking I might see him again and wondering what he'd do. But it was a woman at the counter, and when I hands in the dates of birth she says, 'Ooo, so you're the one that didn't know the dates of birth.' And I thought, Here we go!"

"She goes out and I just stands there waiting for the police. But do you know what?"

"No. What happened, Bert?" Someday, I thought, I'll have to write this down.

"She comes back with all her friends, 'cos they've heard what I done and they wanted to have a look at me!"

"You were lucky, Bert." I said with relief, and could no longer contain my laughter.

The others looked round. "What's he been telling you, Jerry?"

"I was just saying," said Bert, "that I've been all over the world – Japan, Indial, Americal – you name it, and I've been there. And this is the first time I've ever eaten any foreign food."

"What did you eat then, Bert?" someone asked.

"Steak 'n peas 'n chips. That's what the other lads always said, and I'd say, 'Same for me.' I thought it was all you were allowed to have." And after a moment's reflection, "That vindaloo was alright though. I think I'll try that again."

I'm told they've now changed the openings on the Labour Exchange counters. You can no longer thrust your hand through.

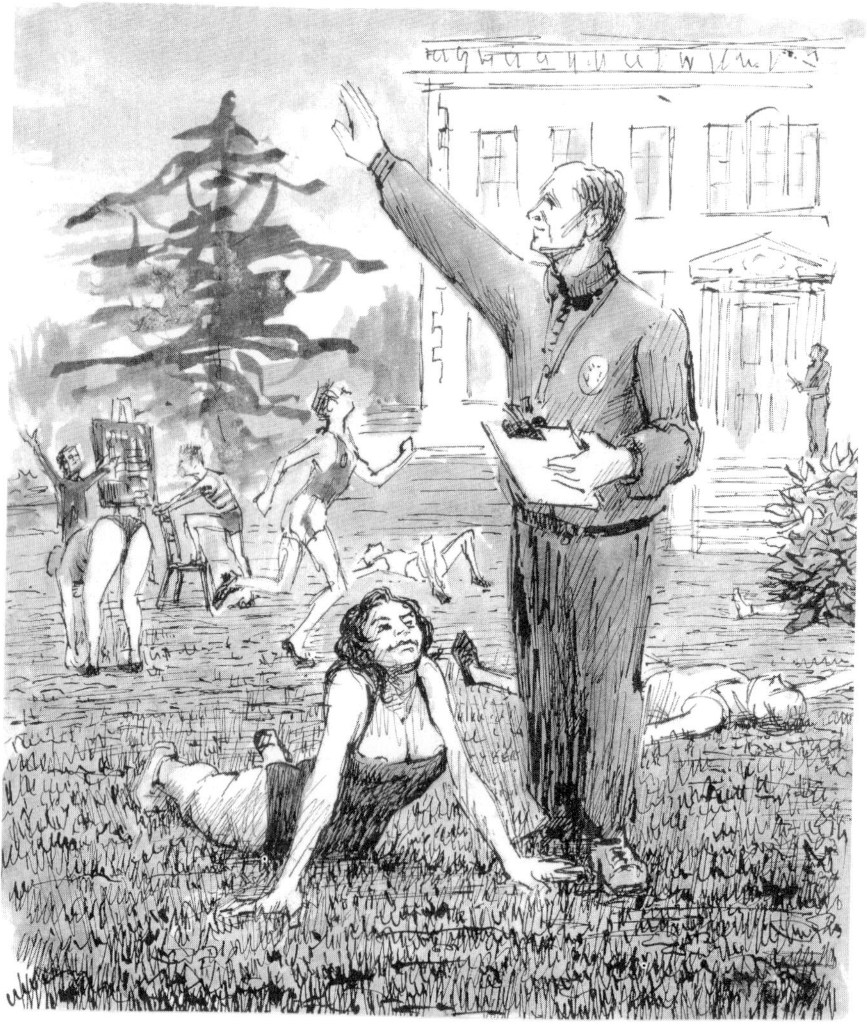

The Caucus Race

*"Why," said the Dodo, "the best
way to explain it is to do it."*

The young couple seated in the far corner of the lounge had not escaped my schoolmasterly vigilance. Always keep a wary eye on the back row. My attention was attracted because, instead of gazing seductively into each other's eyes whilst ostensibly discussing whatever Sports Council course had brought them to the National Recreation Centre at Lilleshall Hall, they were staring fixedly at us.

Our closely knit band of judo coaches were attending our annual conference exotically entitled "The Zadankai"; and we were enjoying a private joke after dinner. Ivan Silver had been innocent enough to ask Ray Mitchell and Harry Welsh if they knew anything about "PFIs"; and our two Army Coaches needed no further invitation to practise their mischievous double act:

"Dear, oh dear, oh dear! What's a PFI?"

"I'm surprised at you Ivan. Aren't you surprised Ray? A Senior Coach should at least know his own Physical Fitness Index."

"We'd better sort that out for him right away. Got your stop watch there Harry?"

After Ivan had scattered the startled peacocks on the terraced lawns as he raced round prescribed circuits, his instructors had returned him to the lounge for step tests and press ups. However, he is nobody's fool; so when, after driving himself to exhaustion, Ivan checked Ray's pulse rate, it was anyone's guess as to who was extracting the Michael from whom.

This spontaneous parody of the latest pseudo scientific pretension was immediately contagious. Our entire group were soon participating with the seriousness of Buster Keaton. It was, presumably, this illusion of academic research which attracted the attention of the two strangers.

Consumed with curiosity, the young man finally approached our theatre of the absurd.

"Excuse me. What exactly are you doing?"

And, without so much as the twitch of a lip, Harry replied:

"Assessing PFIs."

The young man had come in search of wisdom, and by chance had stumbled on a convention of gurus speaking authoritatively about initial letters! He plunged headlong down this rabbit hole of opportunity . . .

"Do you mind if we join in?"

"We'd be glad of your assistance," said Ray; and, without a moment's thought as to where this deception would lead us, we all acquiesced.

For ten years our dedicated group had abandoned wives and families during Whitsun weekend in answer to Geof Gleeson's summons to the serious minded planning of our Association's Coaching Strategy for the following year. Jim Lane, the warden of this Arcadian Shropshire retreat, had long since revised his original conviction that all judo men are lunatics. The occasion when a devout disciple, absorbed in profound conversation with the founder, had inadvertently wandered into the lily pond was now seen as a freak aberration. With characteristic courtesy, Jim granted us use of the staff room for relaxation, and a lasting friendship had blossomed.

In these circumstances how could we have encouraged a private joke to escalate into the outrageous fraud that overtook the entire establishment? You may well ask; and I am as perplexed as anyone. It seems that cloistered males occasionally revert to absurd irresistible impulses. We make apple-pie beds, roll up our trouser legs, sing vulgar songs and defy Black Rod. These boisterous rituals are not as sinister as the fiery crosses and Mafia initiations of our foreign counterparts, but they puzzle our wives. Even in maturity we cannot resist a practical joke – especially when unsolicited victims present themselves!

However, I recount the shameless events which ensued at Lilleshall, less as a celebration of judo pranksters, than as a cautionary tale of astonishing public credulity.

April 1st, never saw the like; and never will – without a full day's extension. Candid cameras never count victims by the score; and only carefully planned academic hoaxes have exploited intellectual pretension with comparable audacity. The extraordinary self delusion which overtook Lilleshall carried the deceits of professional sport into the realms of the Emperor's clothes which adorn contemporary art. PFI gobbledegook anticipated by twenty years the explanations delivered on TV by participants in the gigantic 1992 German Exhibition of Art and Sport. On that occasion even the worldly Sheena McDonald appeared beguiled by the metaphysics:

"We need to animate space with people – pose the universal question, 'What's going on here?' – in a way humorous – folly of trying to contain nature – INTERVENE – follow an impulse – what would happen if I jumped into the water? – recently I've been crossing the road more often – Man, there's no boundary to Art!"

Within half an hour of the intrepid sports couple asking the universal question, "What's going on here?" an avalanche of Lilleshall weekenders ingenuously volunteered to, "animate space with people." The total ground floor space of the Stately Home pulsated with the fervent groans of athletes in search of a PFI.

Our coaches accepted "the folly of trying to contain nature" and "followed an impulse". They "intervened" on the dance floor and quickly replaced bewildered dancers with sporters pressing down floors and stepping up on chairs – indefinitely.

The first PFI participant to collapse was carried to the sanatorium – from whence he sent a touching message of apology for expiring, and gratitude for being allowed to take part. Others rushed to take his place as the word was passed:

"The first PFI in the country! A special induction course!"

Jim Lane betrayed no hint of his mystification. The fabric of the building was undamaged; and eventually everyone tottered off to bed – far too exhausted, had they been so minded, for fornication.

Breakfast was animated by discussions of the evening's unexpected excitement. I "intervened" with the following announcement:

"In response to overwhelming requests for more accurate PFI assessments, the British Judo Coaches are prepared to suspend their morning session and accommodate all who wish to continue with our pilot study. Those wishing to actively participate should forgo breakfast and assemble on the lawn in half an hour."

Loath to see good food wasted, we ate heartily, and presently emerged into the sunlight with all the paraphernalia of "experts" – clip boards, pencils, stop watches and whistles; and also a large blackboard on which to collate data.

About one hundred eager participants were gathered amongst the flower beds – impatient young footballers boasting squad track suits and accompanied by lugubrious trainers – those whom we uncharitably called "The Keep Fat Ladies" constrained in resilient leotards – suave squash players affecting silk scarves – lean athletes pared down to shorts and vests – and, rather alarmingly, a number of professional coaches anxious to be initiated into the latest trend in the "race for supremacy".

If I was momentarily troubled by the vision of a stately lynching party, I quickly found reassurance in the fighting record of my fellow conspirators. In any case the die was cast.

Under the fascinated gaze of our trusting audience we arranged chairs in complex configurations with exaggerated exactitude. The blackboard was divided into vertical and horizontal columns, each headed by arbitrary initials or symbols. Ray and Harry delivered a few confidential words of guidance with quiet authority, made fleeting reference to the hieroglyphics on the board and directed the excited rabble to various stations amongst the circuit of chairs.

"No need to worry about technicalities" was the final instruction. "Leave that to us. Just do what you can."

Thus began the Caucus Race. When whistles blew some started, some stopped, some changed stations, some ran, some rested, some stepped, some pressed – and some lost their way in the rhododendrons. "Man, there's no boundary line to Art."

And amidst all the jerking and curling and squatting and thrusting our lynx-eyed coaches made "expert" assessments. We seized unexpected moments to check pulse rates, note times of seemingly inconsequential events and record undisclosed data on our clip boards. From time to time we shouted to the recorder manning the blackboard such messages as:

"Fifty two point seven over here."

"A rising pulse rate of one twenty."

And to the amazement of all contributors the board was gradually covered with signs and numbers of no significance whatsoever.

Inevitably there were questions – not the universal one, "What's going on here?" But breathless apologetic questions from the curious, the nervous, the wary and the erudite; naive questions to excuse incompetence and astute questions to demonstrate the complete comprehension of a fellow "expert". We were never short of an answer.

"Do you really think I'm fit enough to undertake this sort of thing?"

"Do exactly what you can Madam, and your score will be multiplied by the FVF – Fitness Variability Factor."

"I'm afraid I can't do press ups. Does that invalidate my score?"

"Press ups and squat thrusts are interchangeable according to your respiratory cardiovascular responses."

And then the professional coach's clever question: "I wonder if you can explain a small technicality. After every station I have to turn to the right – I'm left handed! Surely that will give an inaccurate measurement?"

"You're a coach yourself, are you Sir?"

"Yes. How did you know?"

"Well it's a very good question. Absolutely vital. You see that man standing over there with the clip board? No, right over there by the house. Yes? Well, its his special job to take account of exactly that deflection."

"Astonishing!"

"Well we can't leave anything unaccounted for, can we now?"

It was stimulating to observe how long they maintained their exertions; but gradually the faint hearted and the utterly exhausted collapsed into chattering huddles.

"Well, that's my lot. I can hardly move a muscle."

"It does go to show though, doesn't it?"

"Oh, it certainly does. You never really know till you start to measure it."

"Once it gets properly established, I'm sure it will make an enormous difference."

"You can bet they've been doing it behind the Iron Curtain for years."

"Well at least we've made a start."

"Are you going to introduce it at your club then?"

"Course I am. Now it's here, we've just got to get on with it."

The hard cases drove themselves remorselessly, until they too conceded they had come to a standstill.

"Very intensive, isn't it?"

"We should have got onto this years ago."

If anyone had requested a personal evaluation, the answer would probably have been: "Purely a pilot scheme, you understand. It would be a little premature etc. etc." But, quite incredibly, no one asked! They were satisfied to have drunk from a little bottle marked 'DRINK ME' in the touching faith that something magical would happen."

However a climax was required because, as the Dodo said, "Everyone has won and everyone must have prizes." What better prize than to be photographed with a team of "experts"? The suggestion was eagerly applauded, and a group picture was taken in front of the blackboard. It was subsequently published, quite innocently, in the judo magazine together with an ambiguous account, which only the initiated could penetrate, of how the Association's Area Coaches had once again led the field by introducing the PFI to Lilleshall.

No one was discomforted by a cry of "Ever been had?" The hoax was never disclosed. Had we been exposed, I'm not sure whether Jim would have chuckled or banned us from Lilleshall – perhaps both! I'm glad he was spared the dilemma.

Very occasionally, when I cringe with embarrassment at the memory of incomprehensible activities I have obediently undertaken at the behest of a judo "expert" it is comforting to recall that the mesmeric tyranny of expertise extends far beyond Oriental cults.

In many sports, totally irrational training, promoted "on expert advice" has heaped absurdity on absurdity. These perverse endeavours often derive from cranky educationalists who oscillate between obsession for measuring everything and fear of measuring anything; from dotty dietitians fully convinced that yesterday's dogma was a recipe for starvation; and from crafty chemists pedalling performance drugs at the expense of health and sexual differentiation.

Some of these gurus have a marginal knowledge of what they are doing; and this small foothold in reality lends credence to their dangerous nonsense and excuses the gullibility of their victims. The Lilleshall Caucus Race had no such foothold. It was a deliberate spoof – "in a way humorous".

But no doubt there are still clubs about the country where a revered coach expounds to his credulous charges the value of an accurate PFI:

"In fact I helped pioneer this science at Lilleshall where I was privileged to assist a group of experts."

Recently I've been crossing the road more often.

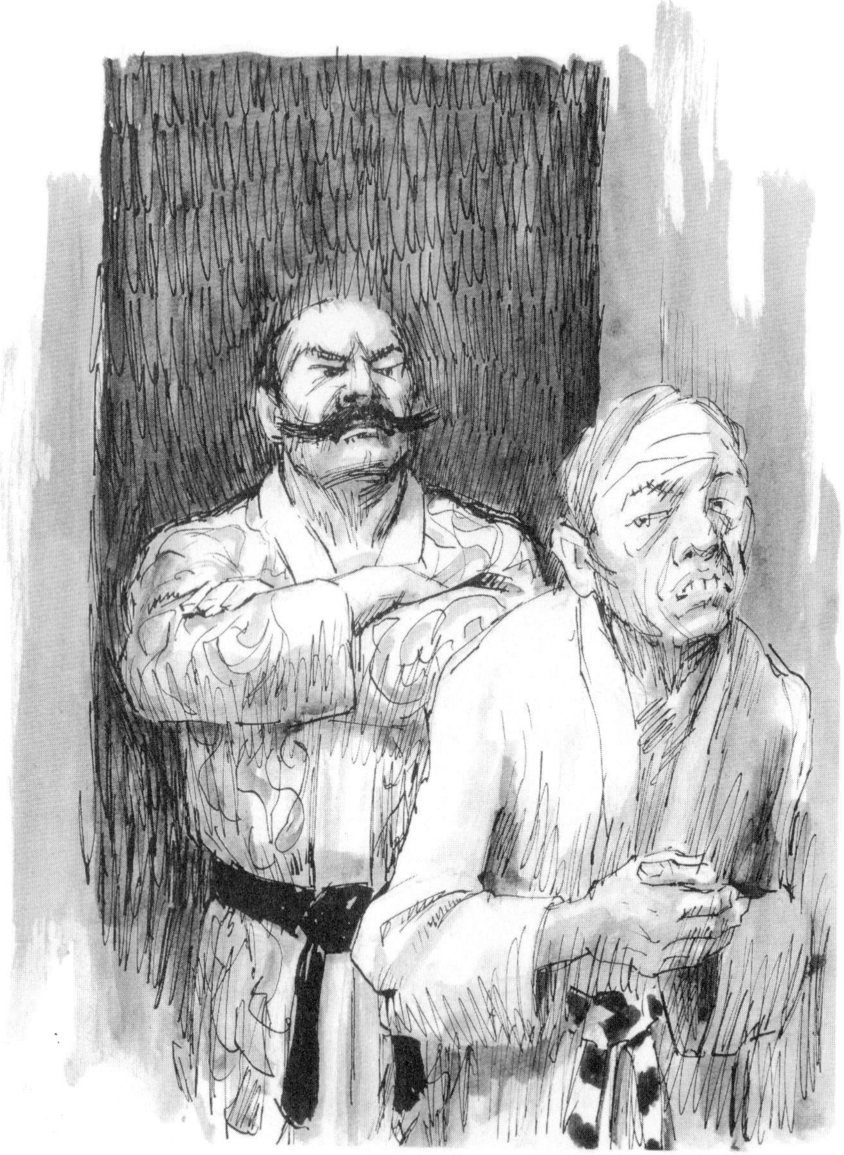

The Man who Bit the Belt

"The time has come," the Walrus said,
"To talk of many things –
Of shoes – and ships – and sealing wax –
Of cabbages and kings."

"I don't suppose you ever met the man who bit the belt?" I asked Geof, half expecting to have another illusion shattered.

During our friendship since his return from Japan I frequently probed his experience for insight into the birthplace of judo. "Did you have a chance to practice with any of the very old 10th. dans?" I once inquired, because I'd seen a film in which one of them, at the age of seventy, threw ten young champions. The irreverent reply had been, "Not me; I wasn't strong enough to hold the poor old fellows up."

On this occasion I wasn't expecting mythology. We were alone in the Staff Common Room at Lilleshall. The other coaches had turned in around midnight. Jim Lane had popped his head round the door and left us to it. The night was still young.

"You've heard about Ushi Jima then?"

I nodded. Trevor Leggett our mutual teacher had recounted to me how this formidable man had won a critical contest in Japan by resorting to a highly controversial expedient. Gripping tightly with both hands, he had secured a winning hold on the ground which his opponent was about to dislodge before the required 30 seconds had elapsed. In desperation Ushi Jima had produced a third hand by seizing the knot of his victim's belt between his teeth and dragging him securely onto his back.

Although this drastic measure was not considered gentlemanly, it was not illegal; so a new prohibition was introduced into the rules and its justification immortalised "the man who bit the belt."

Ushi Jima's indomitable will to win was inculcated into his three remarkable pupils – Kimura, Hirano and Ishikawa. To the fury of the Kodokan, their Svengali like master would announce in advance which one of them would win the annual All Japan Championships. His predictions were never wrong and the victor was usually Kimura, whose prowess was spoken of in awe – even by Leggett:

"I could usually stay up for quite a while against the other two, but there really was no stopping Kimura's o-soto-gari."

When Hirano was given his turn and announced as the forthcoming victor by Ushi Jima, he had the misfortune to break his collar bone and dislocate his shoulder in an early round. "Nothing must stop you," said Ushi Jima as he had repeated a hundred times in training. And, with the broken pieces securely immobilised with strapping, nothing did. He went on to win the final as they say "single handed!"

The master and his terrible triplets became so arrogant that they broke the rules of the Kodokan by forming a professional circus (a familiar story today!). The establishment was at last able to retaliate against years of humiliation and the circus was expelled from the judo fraternity.

Kimura became a professional wrestler in England and America. For a man who could spin his opponents onto their backs at will, it must have been very humiliating to accept his share of pre-arranged losses. Hirano was rescued from an alcoholic decline by the Belgian Judo Association, and Ishikawa went to America. Ushi Jima, left to wander like some "ronin" samurai, was not heard of again – or so I thought until that night at Lilleshall.

"Yes, I met him once," said Geof; and what follows is really his story. I trust he will endorse my performance as his Boswell!

During his four years as an especially privileged foreign member of the Kodokan's research training school, Geof trained six days a week and most evenings at the club's main dojo. In a country where judo flourishes like soccer in England, the club's huge mat area (as big as a large sports hall) was the acknowledged centre of world judo. Training sessions were packed with ambitious international fighting men – predominantly Japanese striving to compete with a host of world champions. The work rate, sweat and concentration were always intense.Only something very exceptional could interrupt this dedicated atmosphere; but one evening the thumps and grunts of a hundred heaving bodies were arrested by an extraordinary loud and persistent noise:

Boom! Boom! Boom!

A thunderous banging on the outer door gradually brought proceedings to a standstill. The noise was especially puzzling as the entrance remained open during practice. Yet the banging persisted. At length an elderly sensei dispatched a lower dan grade to attend to the nuisance.

One can only imagine the young man's shock on being confronted with a fearsome old man who stood motionless with folded arms glaring at him – in total silence! It was Ushi Jima. Like Verrochio's statue of the grizzled old warrior Colleoni his mesmeric stare exuded menace.

Confused by a social situation for which he could recall no appropriate procedure, the young man quickly turned tail and reported the disturbing apparition to an elderly sensei. The old man shuffled towards the door and stiffened with alarm as he recognised the bristling moustache and penetrating eyes of the grim figure who remained unmoved at the entrance.

Almost as rapidly as the youngster he hurried back to the dojo and engaged in earnest discussion with the senior sensei. They must have wished it was their night off! By now an unusual hush had enveloped the dojo, and Geof caught the words "Ushi Jima – Ushi Jima." He wasn't the only one to catch the legendary name, and within seconds an excited buzz spread through the hive:

"Ushi Jima – Ushi Jima – Ushi Jima – Ushi Jima!"

Fortunately the senior sensei recognised the Zen symbolism of knocking at the door. He may even have recalled the poor chap who waited so long for entrance to a monastery that he cut off his arm and sent it in as evidence of his sincerity (Anyone who has sat in hospital casualty reception knows the feeling . . .). Ushi Jima felt he had served his penance and was asking – yes, Ushi Jima who commanded was asking – to be readmitted.

The old sensei went through the ritual and "the man who bit the belt" stalked into the dojo. Disdaining the changing room he stripped the clothing from his tough imperishable old body and donned his well worn judo-gi beside the practice area. As he strode like Rustum into the centre of the tatami the players opened up a respectful space that moved with him as if they were repelled by a magnetic force.

He halted and slowly surveyed the assembled talent, fixing his baleful glare on one young champion after another. Finally a particularly distinguished competitor caught his eye.

"You!" He pointed at his startled choice and indicated a spot on the mats between them. The young man came towards it and bowed to an opponent now in his 60s. After a brief domination of the grips Ushi Jima unleashed a devastating o-soto-gari which recalled Kimura at his best. The old warrior's total commitment carried both to the ground where he immediately secured a powerful unorthodox hold. After a short futile struggle the hapless young champion tapped submission. Whereupon Ushi Jima delivered a ferocious punch to his victim's stomach!

"You!" He selected his next subject for annihilation – and his next – and his next. When there seemed to be no more worthy opponents he directed his malevolent search towards the revered sensei. Although they were many years younger than Ushi Jima there was an unspoken convention that young players invited to practise never threw honourable teachers. (One uncouth Englishman who was not advised of this courtesy popped a very surprised old fellow on his back and was rapidly hospitalised by the sensei's pupils.)

Ushi Jima was absolved from any such constraints by his even greater age. So the ensuing havoc he wrought amongst the sensei was not only a physical assault; it was also an unprecedented blow to the dignity of the hierarchy.

As a final gesture, having established his unassailable authority, the man who had been ostracised for decades and knocked on the door for readmittance clapped his hands and delivered to the world's greatest judo club half an hour's unsolicited instruction. Indomitable pride was at last restored.

Ushi Jima repeated this awesome routine every night for two weeks and Geof watched like some unbidden witness to a violent domestic drama. He even had the temerity to loiter within range of the fearful summons, "You!" And he remembered to tighten his stomach muscles for the inevitable conclusion!

At the end of this sensational fortnight "the man who bit the belt" disappeared into the oblivion from which he had emerged so dramatically, and the Kodokan's bewildered establishment heaved a corporate sigh of relief.

Some months later a watchful sensei rebuked Geof for deploying against a young Japanese a very effective, rough and unorthodox technique.

"But Ushi Jima showed it to me," was his defence.

"Ushi Jima!" The old man almost spat the name – and tottered away in disgust.

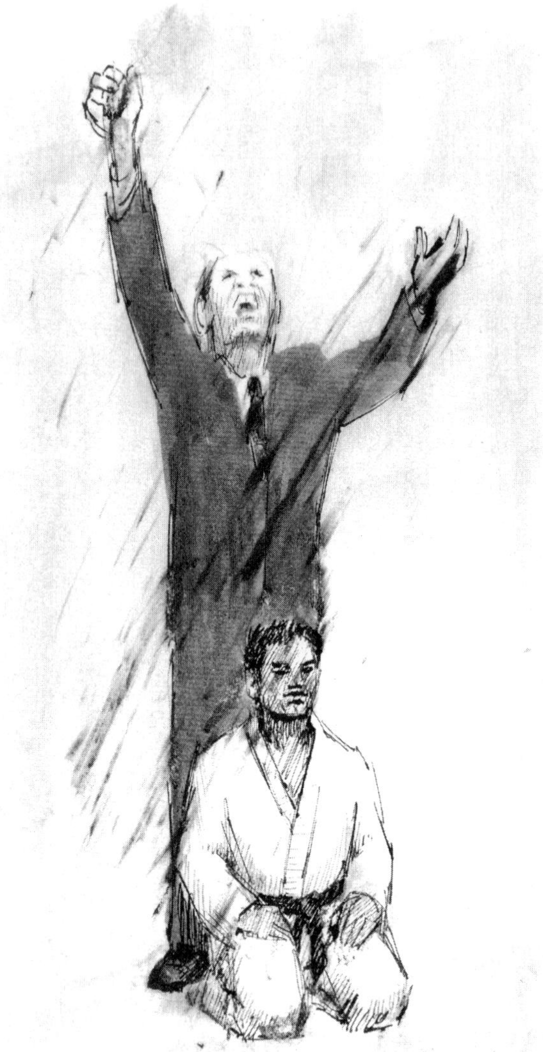

Cultural Collisions

At this moment Five, who had been anxiously looking across the garden, called out, "The Queen! The Queen!" and the three gardeners instantly threw themselves flat upon their faces.

"There are well over a hundred people in this lounge." I explained to my colleagues assembled at Heathrow Airport. "Statistics reveal that one in a hundred passengers using this place lose their luggage. Guess who's going to lose theirs on this trip."

Such pessimistic prognostications received a flippant response from the six senior coaches en route to represent Great Britain at the first International Judo Coaching Conference. In the nine years since Geof Gleeson, our first full time National Coach, had set up a regional net work we had developed an intimate brand of humour and I was ridiculed in the friendliest possible way.

"All right, you laugh," I said with feigned dignity as my bag was sucked into Heathrow's sinister system. "But don't say I didn't warn you."

My Lufthansa flight companion was Ivan Silver who, for a distinguished judo man, proved unusually "faddy" about his diet. Presented with the ubiquitous tray of plastic food substitutes Ivan explained to the Rhine Maiden that, whilst his colleague relished any sort of food, he personally would be grateful if they could find him something more wholesome. She smiled graciously with apparent comprehension, and returned promptly with an identical tray – for me!

This communication debacle was a prophetic prelude to forthcoming absurdities beyond our wildest imaginings.

Luggage was recovered at Frankfurt amidst renewed sidelong smirks, but my neurosis marked me as a seasoned traveller.

"Follow Jerry," shouted Andy Bull, the Scottish coach, as we dashed for a departing train; and Ivan, unnerved by hunger, led the chase. By the time we reached Karlshrue ebullience prevailed. We marvelled at Baroque splendour and the free public transport. (It was not until the end of our week's stay that we discovered ticket machines on the trams.)

Finally a funicular railway which climbed to a picturesque hilltop venue delivered us into the arms of our genial hosts.

"Where's old Goldfinger?" they enquired, and we apologised for the Chairman's absence.

Teutonic organisation dispatched us with presentation briefcases, crammed with programmes and souvenirs, to pristine sleeping quarters.

"Accommodation's a bit rough," said Keith. "No sheets on the bed!"

"You pratt," said Peter in his avuncular way. "These are called Continental Quilts."

Over dinner, which paid homage to grotesque appetites, we were addressed by a VIP whose exact role escaped us. Few of the audience understood his rousing German oratory; so when he soared to an emotional climax the tumultuous applause, cheering and table thumping seemed a little over the top. I was very relieved that none of our high spirited jokers shouted "Zeig Heil!"

The speaker flushed with pride and appeared quite overcome with his rapturous reception. Doubtless he was persuaded that everyone understands good German if it is delivered loudly enough.

Curious as to how the conference lecturers would overcome this linguistic problem, I mentioned the matter to an elderly Dutchman who, like so many of his countrymen, spoke fluent English.

"You are in Germany sir. They have ways of organising these things." But of course – I had forgotten the efficient arrangements for the Nuremburg trials . . .

The opening speaker was our own Geof Gleeson – which was a tribute to the international reputation gained by his remarkable coaching innovations. We had discussed his presentation on the journey and reminded Geof that the effectiveness of his introductory methods would not be believed without a demonstration. So he had agreed to follow his scholarly lecture by conducting a genuine beginners' class, for which our hosts had obtained 12 participants. They have ways of obtaining volunteers.

All seats in the lecture hall were equipped with ear phones providing instant translations by a galaxy of interpreters on a balcony above us. We quickly identified the fraulein serving Britain as the star of the galaxy.

Wolfgang Hoffman, the organiser, whispered to Geof, "I'm relying on you to get it off to a good start. We don't want a repetition of the same old dogma."

I doubt if he realised exactly how iconoclastic Geof's lecture would appear – especially to the illustrious Japanese representatives. Their headquarters at the Kodokan had always been loath to depart by a jot or comma from the teaching of the founder Jigoro Kano as the oldest members remembered it; and Matsumoto who led their delegation was a pillar of the establishment. Geof, who had been a distinguished pupil of the Kodokan for four years infused us with enough confidence to evaluate objectively Japanese tradition. Whilst our respect for the pioneering work of Kano was undiminished we had transcended slavish imitation of methods unchanged for 80 years and unsuited to British physique and culture. Paradoxically we sought to restore the founder's search for knowledge.

I suspect that Geof's speech impediment intensified the slow measured authority of his delivery. One body blow after another shattered the shibboleths of breakfalling, static repetition and standardised technique; whilst the audience were uncomfortably aware of a stony faced presence in their midst. The Japanese were not amused.

But it was the demonstration that finally stood tradition on its head. Within 15 minutes a group of beginners were having a go at the sort of throws, evasions and counter throws traditionally reserved for experienced players – and, even worse, they were enjoying it! Ivan Silver and I compounded this with the ultimate sacrilege of demonstrating an alternative version of the ritualistic Nage-No-Kata (15 fundamental throws). Graffiti on a war memorial would have been more acceptable to the traditionalists.

In the afternoon a German psychologist visibly bursting with brains, and without any prior collaboration, confirmed the Gestalt and other principles previously enunciated by Geof. Only iron discipline prevented the stony expressions from disintegrating. The British coaches, swept along on a tide of euphoria, asked a string of academic questions whilst the Japanese were ominously silent. Sacred cows were dashing for cover.

With a final thrust, worthy of Brutus, Geesink paid a handsome tribute to Geof – a respected opponent in their competitive days. If Matsumoto was a symbol of Japanese judo, Geesink was the European standard bearer; for he had taken both the World and Olympic heavy and open weight competition titles from the Japanese. Matsumoto would need to pull a tiger out of the oriental hat if his lecture on the following day were to restore the Kodokan's previously unquestioned authority.

Dinner was another milestone in my eating life. Over coffee we tried to fraternise with those deprived of the English language; but the conversational limitations of judo terminology and scribbles in my sketch pad eventually reduced us to a nationalistic huddle in one corner of the bar. This was unexpectedly penetrated by a messenger with the differential demeanour of Boris Karloff. He requested that

Mr Gleeson and his two senior coaches should attend a private meeting with the Japanese delegation – at once.

Geof, Harry Welsh and I, agog with curiosity, were led to a small room where, for some unaccountable reason, the lights were dimmed. Was this perhaps a ritualistic requirement of some unspeakable ceremony of retribution? Would Geof be excommunicated for his blasphemous lecture and cast out from the judo fraternity like Ushi Jima until the passing of years permitted a ceremonious knock on some establishment door and request for readmittance? Would Harry and I be banished for complicity?

These absurd fantasies were arrested by the entrance of Matsumoto escorted by German and Japanese deferential minions. There was no muffled gong nor prostrate bows – though Matsumoto's bearing suggested that there should have been. His tall imposing figure discouraged back slapping introductions. Chumminess was not the key note. An awkward silence was prolonged by confusion as to which language should launch proceedings.

The obvious solution was for Matsumoto to address Geof directly since the latter speaks fluent Japanese and could have translated to us. However, after some furtive discussion in the Kodokan camp, it was decreed that a German speaking Japanese would translate Matsumoto's words to an English speaking German who in turn would translate to the British coaches – devilish ingenuity!

We shrugged our shoulders in bewildered compliance and the two Germans looked as apprehensive as the Red Queen's gardeners caught painting white roses red. Some guttural protestations suggested Matsumoto was unhappy to take the initiative, but realising there was no alternative he finally framed a sentence. Geof understood immediately but we had to endure two stages of translation by Bill and Ben before the question was delivered:

"Mr Matsumoto wishes to know what questions will be asked by the British coaches after his lecture tomorrow?"

We were momentarily dumbfounded and could think of no more sensible reply than, "It depends on what Mr Matsumoto has to say."

Bill and Ben exchanged terrified glances but, when the garden failed to swallow them up, the answer was relayed back to Matsumoto. He stood for some time in silent contemplation. Had he not yet prepared his lecture, or was he loath to disclose its content in advance? We waited. Finally he nodded without a word and stalked out – followed by his obsequious retinue. Tantantara Zing Boom!

"What was it all about then?" asked Peter Barnett and the others; and Geof, who has some insight into the Oriental Mind, said:

"The Japanese are scared stiff, so go easy on the questions tomorrow lads. Give them an easy ride."

Matsumoto approached the rostrum without a written text. His measured tread suggested the fortitude of Sidney Carlton approaching the guillotine. He stared at the wooden roof for so long that the audience began to follow his gaze as if fearful that he had discovered some structural defect. Quite suddenly he spoke, and almost immediately our headphones were activated.

"Mr Matsumoto says that out of the free flow of movement comes judo. (Does that sound right?)" We signalled to our galactic star with upraised thumbs.

Matsumoto then indicated to a recent world lightweight champion called Ishi that a demonstration was needed. Ishi bowed in all directions including his partner's and commenced some fluid non competitive free practice. When he had exhausted his elegant repertoire of throws he cast an inquiring glance at Matsumoto. Ten minutes gone – thirty to go . . .

The Kodokan standard bearer realised something more was required. He motioned Ishi to sit down and reclaimed the microphone. There followed another excruciating pause before he spoke.

"Mr Matsumoto says judo is . . . force? (Is that the right word?)"

The tentative translation was dramatically confirmed by Matsumoto who abandoned technology and was now shouting at us – in English!

"Yes, force – FORCE!"

He searched round desperately for some means of emphasising his thesis and alighted on a large piece of chalk alongside the blackboard. This was not a stick but a substantial two inch cube. He grasped it firmly in his right hand and found himself standing behind Ishi who was sitting on his heels in correct kata posture.

We waited with nervous apprehension whilst Matsumoto sought another revelation from the roof; but the inspiration he sought was at his feet. As his gaze fell on Ishi his silent prayer was answered. He raised his clasped hand majestically above his head, From his lower abdomen he expelled one final cry of, "FORCE!" and with all the power of a past champion he hurled the chalk down on Ishi's head!

With his back turned to Matsumoto the little judo man had no warning. The block shattered on impact. His eyes bulged. His body lurched and almost keeled over. The astonished audience gave an involuntary gasp; but almost immediately, when it was apparent that Ishi was still conscious, the tension snapped. They exploded into a riotous acclamation of applause and laughter. It was uncomfortably reminiscent of their response to the German orator.

And suddenly Matsumoto knew he was reprieved. He had hit the right note, or to be precise the right head. It was over. Anything more would be an anti climax. He bowed to the audience and for the first time during the conference he smiled.

The rest of the week was a riot of good food, wine tasting in the Black Forest, twenty a side football organised by Peter Barnett, dancing with the galaxy, cementing friendships, arranging exchange visits, flogging other people's judo kit to the Israelis until the owners found out and even the odd lecture. Mr Matsumoto made a public apology for the inadequacy of the Japanese contribution and promised to do a lot better next time; but there never was a next time.

We alighted on Heathrow late at night, and after standing around a carousel for 20 minutes acknowledged the sad realisation that everyone's luggage, crammed full of souvenirs and presents, had been lost!

"Jerry put a jinx on it," said Andy, and humour was restored. Perhaps the wretched musician who lost his luggage in "Death in Venice" would not also have lost his reason had he joined a jocular judo club.

I made one hell of a fuss, by-passed protesting underlings and harassed the silver haired head of B.E.A. into phoning Frankfurt. Eventually he received confirmation that all our possessions had been found intact.

In response to the "Customary" question, "Anything to declare?" I said, "Yes – I declare you've lost our luggage."

"I wish I had a pound for everyone who told me that," was the quick retort. And then I saw that the questioner was holding a large piece of chalk in his hand. He must have wondered why I began to laugh rather hysterically. Another drunken hooligan!

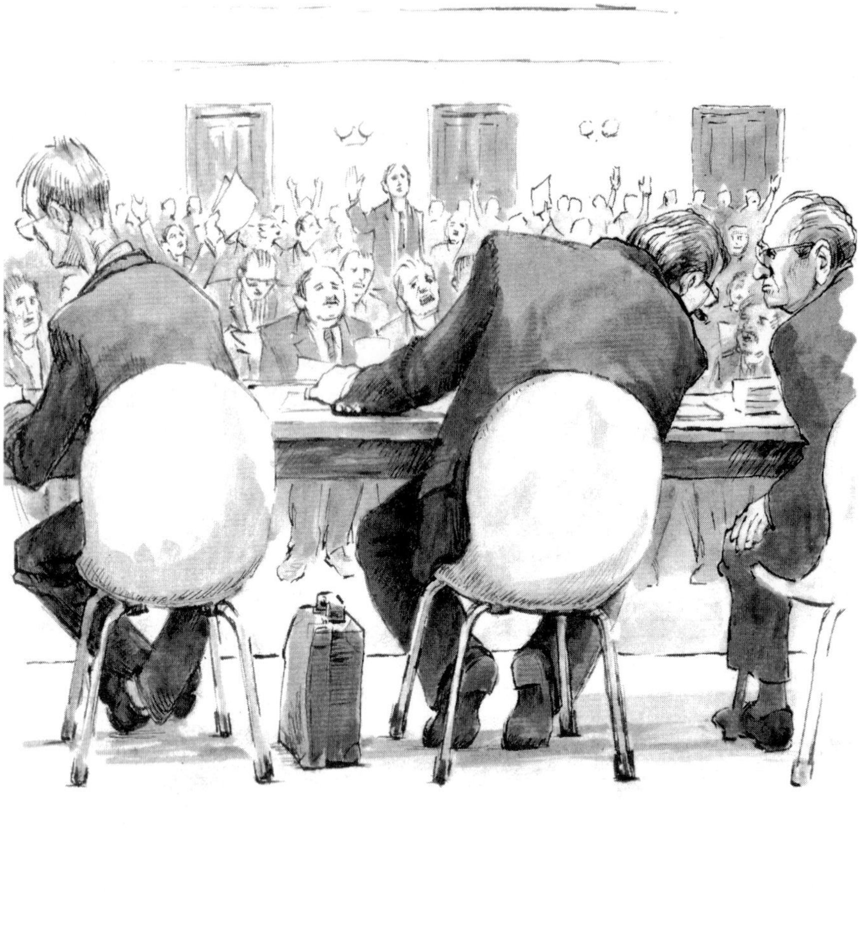

Drake's Drum to the Sound of One Hand Clapping

I sent to them again to say,
"It will be better to obey."
The fishes answered with a grin,
"Why what a temper you are in!"

Spud Murphy still speaks with pride of the day in 1969 when he and I had our judo licences withdrawn. These were not licences to kill, as rumoured by squeamish observers at the time; but national membership documents of the British Judo Association – (BJA for short).

Ironically, the Individual Licence Scheme had been invented by Spud, our Western Area Chairman, as a means of placing the national organisation's precarious finances on a firm foundation. The BJA grasped this lifeline, survived, flourished and then suffered an insidious shift towards centralisation. A paid national licensing officer replaced the regional volunteers, and before long a secretary and typists were added to the pay roll. Eventually BJA Headquarters decided to increase their share of the licence fee at the expense of the Areas.

The West, England's largest geographical area, was particularly hard hit, but for once Spud's belligerence was of no avail.

"Better get Jerry Hicks to write a letter to the Prime Minister," he finally suggested.

In the event it was agreed that I should write, on behalf of the West, to the newly appointed Sports Minister, Dennis Howell, and ask if it was proper for a Sports Council grant to be largely spent on a handful of office workers. And in due course an apprehensive Sports Council officer was dispatched to confront the BJA Chairman who ruled like a Mikado.

"The West are questioning Our Judgment!" One can imagine the bellowing rebuke. "Who the hell do they think they are?"

In recent years the West had not endeared themselves to Headquarters. A desk in London can instantly convert a back slapping, beer swilling sportsman into a gauleiter and a jolly judo prankster into a Fulham Road Shogun. Our provincial irreverence for such pretensions would have been overlooked if we had not been so infuriatingly enterprising: Inter Area Competition – support for

Gleeson's heretical coaching – promotion of a British Schools Judo Association (which played judo for fun!) – experiments with hallowed rules. Such pioneering endeavours were not required of subservient satellites. They were a constant source of irritation. And now this! A letter to a Minister! Who the hell do we think we are?

During his monthly eight hour committee meeting in London the Mikado was offered a tempting remedy for these turbulent minions by one of his Shoguns: If the West's elected committee were dissatisfied, Headquarters should remove them from office; and if Murphy and Hicks were the articulate ringleaders of an uprising they should be silenced by expulsion. Robespierre suffered a similar fate.

A demonstration of absolute authority proved irresistible. Spud and I received expulsion notices and the Area committee were sacked! This was the Shoguns' first mistake.

All Western Area clubs were then summoned to a meeting in Bristol with the BJA committee for the appointment of "an acceptable area committee". This was their second mistake. The entire west country shares 20,000 Cornishmen's rejection of domination by London grokels. Territorial invasion and orders to replace our elected members were tantamount to a declaration of war.

At 13.50 hours on November 15th. the Mikado's army arrived in Bristol and trooped triumphantly towards the Unicorn Hotel. Passing them on the threshold, my wife was overcome by an unaccountable surge of charity:

"I hope it won't be too bad for you," she murmured.

The unnerving effect of this encounter with a soothsayer was reinforced almost immediately as they entered the conference room and found themselves in the midst of a crowded hostile meeting of the revolutionaries – already in progress! We had hired the room for the morning and received a heartening response to a rallying campaign which we christened "Drake's Drum".

Extensive phone calls had summoned an angry horde of current members, and also roused from retirement distinguished veterans who had risen, since our age of innocence, to become District Councillors, Senior Civil Servants, Headmasters, Senior Lecturers and the like. They did not suffer London's delusions of grandeur gladly.

When I phoned Keith Menadue, he said, "We remember the BJA Chairman. He walked on our mats with his shoes on. Cornwall don't forget. We'll be there Jerry." They were; and so were Devon, Dorset, Somerset, Wiltshire, Gloucester and Bristol. It only needed our wives to bring their knitting . . .

Ray Brooks acted as chief negotiator, and refused to open discussions until Tim Collins of the South West Sports Council was accepted as a neutral chairman. Tim's unparalleled act of heroism has become a cautionary legend amongst his Sports Council colleagues. Accepting his appointment was the Shoguns' third mistake.

The fourth may have been to admit Spud and me as "silent observers"; but our presence made little difference. We both watched with pride as Ray and Councillor Don Gough, with massive coordinated support, ran legalistic rings round the opposition.

Tim finally said with weighty authority, "It seems there will be no resolution until Messrs. Hicks and Murphy are reinstated." The Mikado threw in the towel and then the entire Western Area Committee were reinstated.

We had a party that evening, and celebrated with fireworks previously purchased in a wave of optimism. Defectors from the invading army, who had been out voted on the expulsion order, joined us, and the camaraderie bubbled over.

However the original bone of contention, our usurped funds, still lay in the jaws of Headquarters. So the West followed 20,000 Cornishmen to London. To be precise, we travelled in a hired coach to the BJA Annual General Meeting. And accompanying the rebels was George Cooksley, the West's senior yellow belt. He proved to be an unexpected secret weapon.

George had received a severe blow on the head as a youngster and he explained to me, "I'm a bit slow in picking things up; but if you don't mind teaching me I'm prepared to stick at it."

"Persistence," I said with complete sincerity, "is more valuable than talent."

Over many years George became a landmark in the West – always happy to drive those like myself without personal transport, and willing to travel miles off the route to any cafe where the tea was two pence cheaper. His progress to the first grade of yellow belt was painfully slow; but he never missed a training session, an instructional course or an incomprehensible foreign judo book. On this occasion he knew where his duty lay.

To recover our half share of regional income we needed to demonstrate to the General Meeting that financial difficulties at Headquarters were due to mismanagement and our complaints to the Minister fully justified. On a highly elevated rostrum the Chairman had marshalled in defence: the treasurer, his legal adviser, a Sports Council officer and a somewhat irrelevant Marquis of Queensbury. Perhaps the last was to bring Gilbertian pomp and ceremony to the proceedings.

"Bow, bow ye low and middle classes . . . Tantantara Zing Boom!"

Questions on the accounts came with growing impatience from the West's Major Bricknell and other financial experts. But the defence was resolute. Every thrust was skillfully parried. The West were growing desperate.

Then, to our astonishment, George, who rarely spoke at meetings, stood up and raised his hand.

"Yes? State your name and which club you represent." The chairman drew intimidatingly on his cigar.

"Cooksley. Weston YMCA." George didn't flinch.

"Do you wish to ask a question?"

George paused before replying. His lack of total comprehension, evident to those who knew him best, was mistaken on this occasion for owlish inscrutability. What new expert had the West enlisted to embarrass the establishment?

"Yes," replied George at length. "I do wish to ask a question."

"Well what is it?" said the Chairman guardedly.

These circuitous preliminaries had caused a hush to descend on the boisterous assembly. The establishment on the rostrum looked furtive. George's silent scrutiny was unnerving. Then it came:

"What about the badges?"

The Chairman's expression almost imperceptibly froze, like that of a poker player who's been called with nothing in his hand. George had inadvertently opened a Pandora's box. The dark emotions which can be unleashed by badges are entirely disproportionate to their overt importance. It is their symbolic significance which is multi faceted.

Badges for what? Club, County or National badges? Worn on judo-gi in dazzling unlimited array, or restricted in number? But restricted by whom and with what authority? Badges on track suits, ties, T shirts, trophies, ash trays, letterheads or funeral cards? Badges for children to raise funds? Badges for officials to validate fees? Badges which infringe patent laws, breach heraldic rules or incense the Triads? Badges which provoke protracted law suits?

George was oblivious to all these explosive issues. His innocent and irrelevant enquiry could have been unravelled quickly by a less guarded response. But the Chairman was under fire and thinking 20 moves ahead. He turned to the treasurer and, in an undertone, invited him to answer the question. The treasurer blanched and hedged. A silent appeal to the legal adviser was met with a dismissive shrug, and the Sports Council Officer kept his eyes on the desk. It was hardly a case for the Marquis of Queensbury.

"Would you mind repeating the question?" The Chairman used a standard ploy.

"No," said George deliberately, "I wouldn't mind." Another long unblinking pause.

"Then will you do so?" Controlled desperation!

"Yes." Undertones of a Zen confrontation.

"What was it?" The Chairman was exercising enormous control, but he'd met his match.

"What about the badges?"

The badges, the badges, those blasted badges! The Chairman wavered for an instant and the audience sensed a chink in the hitherto impregnable armour:

"Answer the question." shouted Charlie Gardner, Judokwai's secretary and a trebuchet expert.

"Yeah, the question!" roared John Cronin and other hard men from the Star club.

"Answer the question." echoed the descendant of a Cornish wrecker.

A dozen bellicose voices took up the cry:

"Answer the question. Answer the question."

It was some time before order was restored. The confusion, skillfully exploited by the West, was not even unravelled – let alone resolved. This confirmed the growing suspicion of a "cover up" – which may well have existed; but not about the badges!

The West's proposal for a restoration of 50% of the licence income to the Area was put to the vote and carried unanimously. The establishment did not relish another altercation.

As we drove back along the A38 "Westward, westward, always westward, to the setting of the sun" someone shouted, "Well done George!"

George gave a shy grin. "I think I'm going to donate a trophy for the best yellow belt in the West."

Alas! Before George could compete for the Cooksley Shield he was unexpectedly promoted to orange belt. And it didn't stop there! Against every prediction he doggedly mastered a single trick on the ground which eventually earned him enough points for his black belt.

GK often quoted, "The wise man can learn more from the fool than the fool can learn from the wise." This Oriental aphorism acquires added piquancy when the roles are interchangeable.

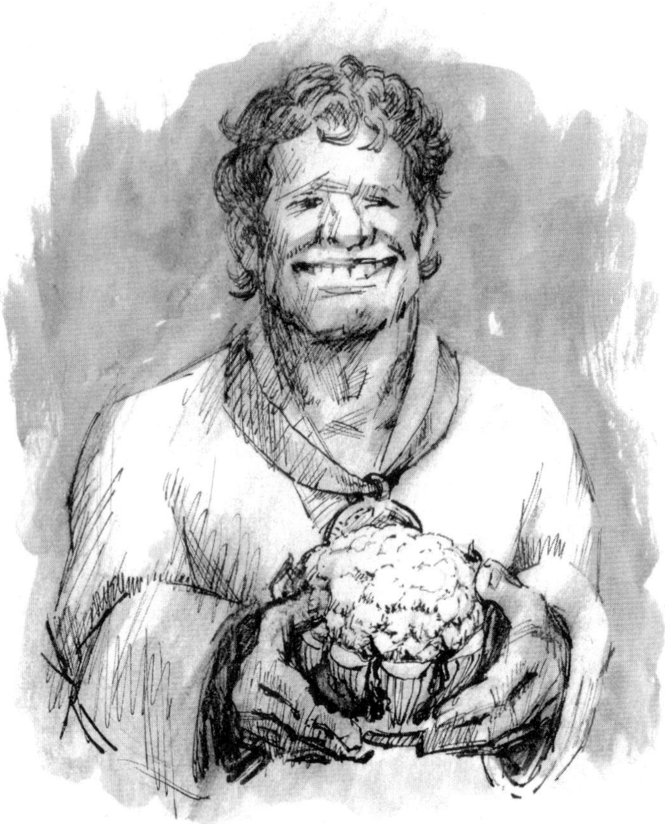

A Bunch of Five

Alice thought the whole thing was absurd — she simply bowed and took the thimble looking as solemn as she could.

When Danny Da Costa mounted the victor's rostrum at the conclusion of the 1974 British Open Judo Championships, my delight was tinged with a disturbing little quiver of apprehension. Most odd!

During the previous 14 years, during which I had served as the Western Area Judo Coach, medal presentations had never been a cause for alarm. Why now? A coach's work commences months, even years, before the day of competition. Lest their contribution is unappreciated some employ artful means of enlightening onlookers:

"That's my boy up there on the rostrum. Did you see his brilliant throw in the final? We've been working on that together for months."

Such ploys are seldom matched by:

"That's my lad down there in the corner — crying his eyes out. I taught him everything I know and still he loses!"

Geof Gleeson's coaches strove for greater sophistication; and we extended tactical advice far beyond the customary, "Give 'im the nut Alex!" or "Up the middle Brian!"

Yet analysis of the opposition, tactical planning and mat side coaching were the least of my problems during those interminable days at the Crystal Palace. I recently recalled with John Rowe our shared responsibility for school participants: The Dawn Departure . . . South Circular Nightmare . . . Counting Heads on Late Arrival . . . Lost Record Cards . . . Weighing-in . . . Shedding Weight . . . Warming-up . . . Cooling-down . . . Checking Pool Sheets . . . Recounting Heads. Then hours of tedium on benches designed for galley slaves, exacerbated by Hunger, Thirst and Asphyxiation by chlorine fumes from 3 adjacent swimming pools. First-timers slowly shrivel with anxiety. And then, minutes before The Call For All Competitors To Report (to one of five indistinguishable contest areas) the old-timers all slope off! Similar panic recurs for nine or ten hours and Counting Heads is finally abandoned in despair.

The medal ceremony means all the hassle is over. . .time for the coach to cease Counting Heads, sheep and elusive blessings or expostulating with what he has come to believe are erratic, biased and deranged officials over their incomprehensible decisions . . . time to relax whilst the winners supplement the mantleshelves and trophy cabinets of their fervent parents.

The closing routine was entirely familiar. I missed some of the most prestigious occasions when our Bristol progeny, Nick Strang, Mike Concannon, David Vale and Tony Sweeney won medals in Europe and Japan. (A teacher's leave and purse provide mundane obstacles.) Nevertheless, I witnessed their regional and national victories together with those of the Salmon brothers, Jim Pitman and my own son and daughter more times than I can remember. And presentations never went wrong!*

So, now, with the epic battles of the day behind us and my heart once more properly positioned in its rib cage, why was I apprehensive about Danny's moment of glory? Perhaps because over the years I had begun to anticipate his flair for creating incongruous absurdities when least expected . . .

Daniel Roderiquez Gomez Da Costa did not become my awesome "responsibility" until shortly after he won the first British trials held in weight categories. He was, and remains, a lightweight. As a largely self taught, unknown provincial he had the effrontery to beat all the Budokwai lads on their "home turf"; and that was when the London club dominated British judo.

A bewildered referee was too shocked to award the audacious intruder a full score for throwing the favourite, so Danny jumped on his opponent's back and strangled him. Thereafter this became his speciality. Even the most obtuse referees usually recognise a submission or unconsciousness!

As a consequence of this performance our hero fought for Britain; and, on return, he was outraged to see the fraudulent antics of TV wrestlers attract greater popular acclaim than his judo team mates. A more conventional champion might have grumbled in resignation about another of Life's Injustices. "But this was a man of a score."

He publicly challenged any of the professional wrestlers, regardless of weight, to fight him with one arm tied behind his back. It was no idle boast. The same outrageous confidence with which he mounted the stage of The London Palladium in mid performance and joined in a musical number, bore him along. He would have relished acceptance.

---

* At the Belgrade World Judo Championships in 1989, Karen Briggs of Great Britain was presented with a gold medal to the accompaniment of the German national anthem! In an attempt to rectify the gaff, she was asked to remount the winners' rostrum during a subsequent contest whilst the British national anthem was played.

Unfortunately Danny's bravado came to the attention of The British Judo Association's Executive Committee, who summoned him to a meeting in London. Spud Murphy, our regional chairman, doubted if they were as amused as ourselves and advised caution:

"Better get Jerry Hicks to go along with you. If they upset him, he'll write to the Prime Minister."

Danny's father, who signed letters to the press as Baron Da Costa, accommodated the three of us in a London hotel; and, in those bleak days before you could help yourself, he fortified me with two breakfasts. This was the beginning of a life long friendship between the Hicks and Da Costa families, which brought maverick dimensions to judo coaching, family holidays and legalistic advocacy.

We entered the meeting earlier than we were expected; and it was immediately evident that The Executive Committee were not bursting with suppressed merriment. Mustn't poke fun at The Spanish Inquisition, I thought. The Chairman drew us behind closed doors: "We are awaiting the arrival of our legal adviser." He appeared disconcerted.

"Then you must allow us to summon our barrister." I was holding the Prime Minister in reserve.

"That will not be necessary, Mr Hicks. We only wish to protect Mr Da Costa's interests."

"In that case . . ." I said, rather than, "Pull the other one." And we negotiated. Finally it was agreed that no disciplinary action would be taken if I agreed to "refrain from shouting at the Executive". On a previous visit I had apparently disrupted the tranquillity of a ten hour meeting.

The Committee were not privy to this extraordinary agreement, and were understandably mystified when our reappearance heralded a non event. Their lugubrious lawyer eventually arrived, unencumbered by a sense of fun or any knowledge of the Chairman's tactical withdrawal. He attempted some motion of censure for Mr Da Costa's disregard of judo tradition; but my sharp reminder that GK, the father of British Judo, and Yukio Tani, "a name to conjure with", had both fought professional wrestlers curtailed these uninformed ramblings. Lack of support from Chairman or Committee left him bemused as to the reason for his summons. We quickly expedited our departure from a bewildered establishment, apparently unscathed.

However we left with an uneasy feeling that, in certain select circles, Da Costa would be a persona slightly less than grata. This suspicion was reinforced over the following ten years as Danny was passed over for international selection again and again despite repeated national victories. He was said to be "incident prone".

Although Danny is too light hearted to bear a grudge, I suspect he regretted exclusion from the 1974 squad training in Japan. (I still harbour visions of his debut in the Kabuki Theatre!) Both Danny and Bristol's Dave Vale were medalists in the trials, but were replaced in the squad by a Londoner who was not. It may have been a perception of injustice which spurred Danny to the most intense training of his career.

When he stepped naked on the scales prior to the 1974 British Open his resting pulse rate was 42 and he had the phenomenal ability to do 100 dips and one arm chins. Fortified with honey, orange juice and Waltman recording of Villa Rides, he rapidly demolished the international opposition. A surge of British supporters around the lightweight mat were ecstatic; but the squad selectors looked alarmed.

The draw had been seeded so that Danny would not meet his London rival, who had recently returned from Japan, unless they both reached the final. They both did.

By the time their names were called for the last match of the day, the bleak benches of the "Palace" would generally have been almost deserted . . . but Danny was the only provincial fighting for gold. Supporters from the Midlands and the West remained in force.

"Give 'im stick," shouted Peter Barnett, the Midlands Area Coach. We all knew it was Danny Da Costa versus the Establishment.

Danny's disarming smile at the referee and his opponent did not reach his eyes. He bowed, secured concentration with a familiar grasp of his nose, and on the command of "Hajime" quickly obtained his preferred right hand collar hold – a prerequisite for his fastest strangles.

It was an epic contest. The Londoner never gave up. He'd been made well aware of Danny's supremacy on the ground, and after every stumble miraculously regained his feet or moved surreptitiously out of the contest area.

"He's crawling off the mats," yelled the West, in a vain attempt to alert the referee of this infringement of the rules. "Pull him back Danny. Take him in the middle."

And, as if in response to the roaring urgency of the crowd, Danny gained two small scores with Ko-uchi-gari in rapid succession. His opponent fought desperately to match this advantage . . . anything would do . . . he increased the pace and risked a series of "droppers". But Danny rode buoyantly on the crest of the onslaught; and the selectors watched with increasing dismay.

The West and Midlands chanted in unison the diminishing seconds, "Five, Four, Three, Two . . . One!" Time! Danny Da Costa was again the Lightweight Champion of Great Britain. He shook hands before the formal bow, and the smile finally reached his eyes. Then he vanished!

The red carpet was rolled across the mats to the new Olympic style mounting blocks. Danny reappeared and made the ascent. It was then that I had my twinge of Apprehension.

I felt sure a gesture would be irresistible . . . but what sort of gesture? A Harvey Smith would be too vulgar. . . a clenched fist too banal. Surely not an Oscar speech, "I owe everything to my family of 23, my team of psychoanalysts, a mentally disturbed probation officer and, most of all, to the dear officers of our Association who've always done their damndest!" No, that wasn't Danny. But what?

There was something wrong with his appearance. One speaks of "swollen with pride", but his girth seemed to have increased by a yard! And that uncharacteristic poker face. He knew something we didn't.

The chairman approached resplendent in a double breasted, double vented suit, the backs of his hands swinging forward simultaneously. He was accompanied by a glamorous young lady bearing a silver tray of medals. (During the day other medalists had availed themselves of this unexpected opportunity to kiss her). The gold medal was selected and hung round our hero's neck. Then it happened!

Danny seized the chairman's head in both hands, kissed him loudly on the brow and, with a magician's flourish, produced from inside his protruding jacket a reciprocal presentation which he placed solemnly on the silver tray. There was a silent moment of disbelief before the audience collapsed with laughter at the appearance of a large creamy white cauliflower!

This was the inauguration of The Ceremony of the Reciprocal Vegetable. Cauliflowers were still in season a few months later when the European Championships were held in Britain at the Chlorinated Palace.

Despite his earlier exclusion from the squad, Danny was entered as reserve. When the second lightweight fell ill participation by the maverick West Countryman was inescapable. It was a great disappointment to Britain, as host nation, that we won no more than a single bronze medal before the lightweights fought.

The two Russians were favourites in this category; but Danny swept all before him including the feet of the first Russian in the semi final. Having already obtained a small score, he was assailed with mat side advice to defend his fragile advantage. Yet, even as the squad pundits were advocating caution, he levelled the favourite high in the air to win with a maximum "Ippon".

The same heroic tactics lost the final to the other Russian; but a silver medal was the best Britain had ever achieved in the European lightweights. Danny was the star of the sporting press, albeit rechristened as Norman Da Costa.

The international audience were politely puzzled by the cauliflower ceremony:

"Pourquoi le choufleur? Can you explain please?" Dismissive and apologetic replies failed to satisfy.

Eventually an obsequious and ill disguised emissary of the Establishment approached me "en passant" as it were!

"By the way, Jerry, what exactly is the symbolism of the cauliflower?"

I surveyed him in mock disbelief. "You're not from the West Country, are you? Well, if you were, you wouldn't need to ask." And I moved softly away.

Even that wasn't quite the end of the affair. With Danny's inspirational captaincy and David Vale's brilliant support, the West at last had a chance of success in the Inter Area five man team championship. We had not even reached the semi finals in this event since my own captaincy 16 years earlier. Some special impetus was needed to build a team around our two stars; and we found it in Hamburg.

I had made a friend of Gerhardt Alpers at the Karlshrue Coaching Conference, and arranged a tour of the West for his club. To our surprise their humour had a west country warp. "The rest of Germany think us odd. Bloody minded you call it. Well, Morse! Morse! to them." A rapport had been established. Now was the time for a return visit.

We had a foretaste of the week's lunacy every time our group of ten judo men plus my wife and daughter presented passports for inspection. Danny felt obliged to contort his face to match the hideous impersonation of Quasimodo in his photograph. His contortions earned the dry comment, "This could be an expensive joke, Sir."

But the ruse worked. The grotesque image in his passport deflected attention from Danny's alteration to the expiry date! I recalled the phrase "incident prone". Reg Lomax, our team manager, and I began to wonder if we would return with a complete team.

Gerhardt arranged a series of team matches in North Germany and a visit to a Rieperbahn sex show. Danny led his team triumphantly throughout. His presence and European prestige lent credence to the erroneous belief that we were the National Squad. Gerhardt did not enlighten the towns we visited (Morse! Morse!) and our performance rose to match the deception.

Contest nerves were banished by the outrageous exploits of our mercurial captain ... parodying the public statues he scaled ... mistaking mystified strangers for fellow secret agents ... splashing in the wake of a tourist boat clad only in his underpants whilst the stony faced tour commentator maintained an unbroken narrative about more conventional activities in the port. Gerhardt gallantly entertained my family during the red light outing. We later received lurid reports of how Danny emptied the sex show of the heavy breathing orthodox voyeurs who were not in tune with the farcical antics of British audience participation.

"I've seen other sex shows, and am not very interested," said Gerhardt. "But I would like to have seen Danny's reaction."

At a jovial farewell party we asked Rolph, our Barnstaple heavyweight who was a Hamburger by birth, to translate my parting speech. His Teutonic mind had been so unnerved by the week's buffoonery that he suffered an extraordinary mental dislocation. My English words were translated internally into German before he translated them for the audience – back into English! His ponderous echo of my exact words were incomprehensible to the majority, but was accepted as a final English joke. "They have ways of making us laugh."

As the return train pulled out of Hamburg, our hosts rushed forward waving a Union Jack and thrust into Danny's hand a little man made entirely of nuts.

"Humel! Humel!" we shouted like native Hamburgers.

"Morse! Morse!" was their vulgar traditional response.

Two weeks later our re-assembled team and entourage travelled to Edinburgh for the Inter Area Championships in a series of twin sleeper compartments. My daughter, now an ardent "sporter", remarked to the guard that "On the continent they have six in all the carriages."

"Not on this train lassie! Only the married couples."

Andy Bull organised the tournament at Meadowbank with panache. The Piper's Lament, personal gifts for each of Scotland's opponents, individual seats for spectators and a splendid celebration dinner for all participants were a joyful relief from the years spent in the Crystal Maze of Misery.

The Midlands had broken London's domination of this event the previous year, so the competition was wide open. To everyone's astonishment the West reached the final with Scotland. When we were defeated by our generous hosts our euphoria was not diminished. A critical third win by Alan Kimber in the semi final flowed directly from the spirit generated in Hamburg. The West's finest performance brought Danny once again onto the rostrum – to receive another silver medal (which he insisted on draping round my neck!)

However this time Britain's most successful light weight shared equal honours with four team mates. His legendary skill and irreverence had won the affection of the judo world, and a mischievous audience wondered if team events qualified for ceremonial vegetables.

One suspected the chairman was losing his appetite for cauliflower au gratin. He cautiously approached the West's team crammed onto a platform designed for one with a lacertillian eye on their unpredictable captain. They stood awaiting his presentation like so many theatrical applicants for the role of Napoleon, each with one hand inside his jacket. As judo's distinguished OBE dispensed five silver medals, he received, one by one in return, the five components of a bunch of bananas.

Morse! Morse!

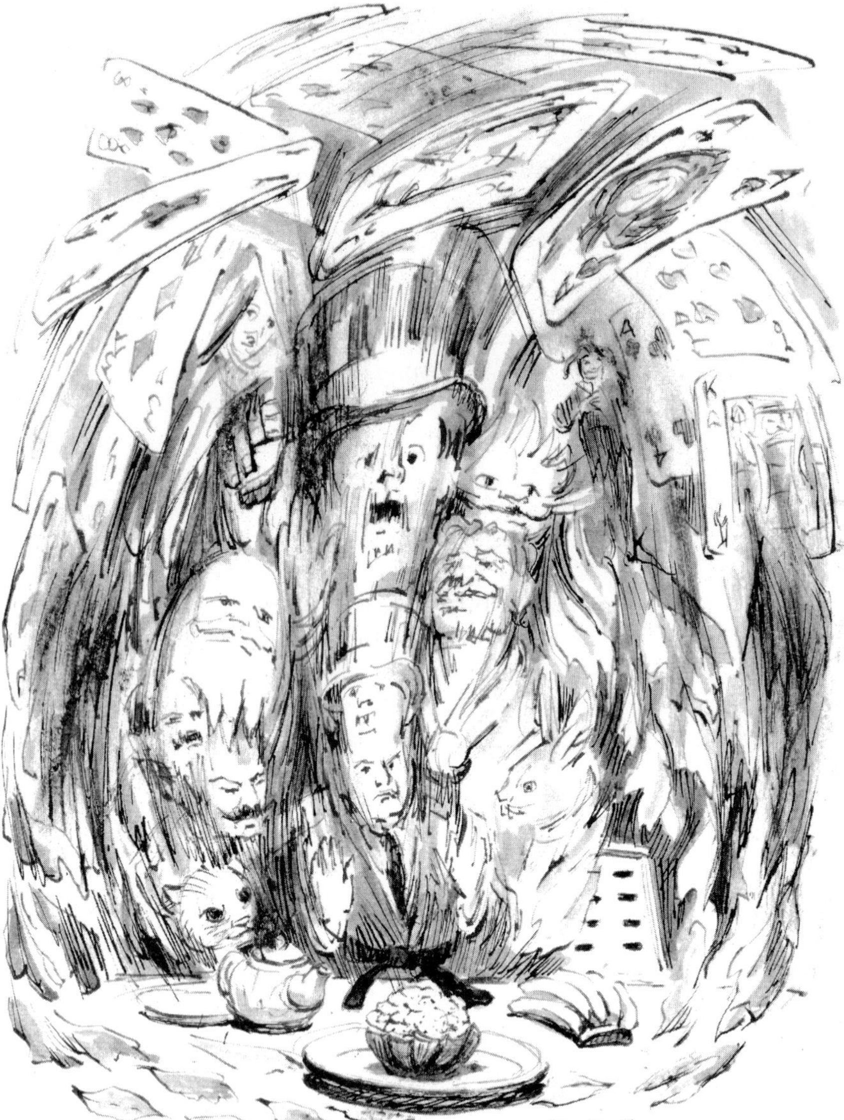

The Trial

The Mock Turtle had just begun to repeat it, when a cry of, "The trial's beginning!" was heard in the distance.

George Yelland received my request for permission to attend a Tribunal with mild surprise. He was a benign headmaster and showed the same indulgence as his predecessor towards my peculiar sport. They were both jealous of Cotham Grammar School's leading role in pioneering and promoting schools judo.

"Not having a brush with the law, Mr Hicks?" he enquired with an arch smile. "Jury service, I presume."

"No. It's an Industrial Tribunal to determine whether the Judo National Coach has been unfairly dismissed. I'm required as a witness for Mr Gleeson."

"Not that charming man who comes to teach our boys? I thought he was quite a celebrity in the coaching world. The P.E. advisers think very highly of him."

"He's a celebrity all right; but too avant garde for our establishment. They find it hard to cope with new ideas that challenge tradition, and Mr Gleeson doesn't suffer fools gladly."

"I thought sport promoted good fellowship."

"I'm afraid, headmaster, that all the wars of Europe started on the playing fields of Eton."

"I think you're misquoting, Mr Hicks."

Geof Gleeson experienced the same difficulties as I in following the basic rules of service which a canny old soldier revealed to me:

"If you want to get on in this Battalion laddie, switch off the radio when the C.O. comes into the Mess, whatever you're listening to; find yourself a cushy number; and always carry some papers when you're skiving off." Good survival advice!

I knew Geof could never be deferential enough to "switch off his radio" for anyone, and retreating into innocuous undemanding work was not his style; but I'd assumed that he had far too much support in the country for the old "Shoguns" to pull off a coup d'état – until I received his phone call:

"Hi, Jerry! How's tricks?"

"OK. What's new?"

"I was asked to attend an E.C. meeting today. A few who seldom turn up had been conscripted; but I'm afraid your chap wasn't there."

"There didn't seem to be much on the agenda."

"There wasn't! So it was quite a surprise when they presented me with my 7th dan for outstanding services to judo – and then gave me the sack!"

"What on earth for?" I was incredulous.

"It was a bit vague. There was a whole list of complaints that no one had mentioned before; but it was a bit difficult to pin them down. I'd written too aggressively to that journalist who claimed I've had no competitive experience; I haven't always been dressed smartly enough; and I wrote to the Chairman in support of the secretary who says he's trodden on. It seems the letter was the last straw."

"Well, we'd better get cracking. Come down to Bristol and I'll introduce you to Paul, a brilliant barrister friend. There are 'Laws of the Land' which even the British Judo Association can't ignore. I'll get onto Spud at once, and we'll see what the Western Area can do. You'll have enormous support outside London."

Spud, the area chairman, was as incredulous as I had been:

"This is going to tear the BJA apart. I'll talk to the other area chairmen, and we'll call an Extraordinary General Meeting. What about a lawyer?"

"Leave that with me Spud; and thanks a lot."

"I'm getting old and tired."

"Aren't we all?"

Paul is a specialist in criminal law, so he recommended a more appropriate colleague who gave us some valuable free advice: Geof should use his union's legal service, but if they didn't employ a barrister we should go back to him. In the event the union hired a corker.

Once the date for the EGM had been fixed, I phoned all the Area Coaches. How many club representatives could they guarantee would attend? It is a long, expensive journey to London for far flung regions, and all the opposition was centred around the capital. So the odds were against us. However clubs were permitted to authorise named representatives from other areas; so if the West, the Midlands and Yorkshire and Humberside could raise surplus supporters, these could vote for Irish and Scottish clubs. We were, as they say, into "a numbers game".

Fortunately we had a "mole" in London who supported Geof. He told me of the strenuous efforts being made to turn every judo group and Evening Class in the capital into a paid up BJA club with voting rights. It was a record growth year for the Association! And the mole kept me abreast of the latest total we needed to exceed.

Geof's team met at the Tribunal offices in Victoria – a drab building in a drab locality for drab cases. Our barrister explained that the opposition would make their case for instant dismissal and he would cross examine. We would then field witnesses, including Geof, to contest their case, and they would cross examine. However he obtained permission for Jim Lane to give his evidence first, due to his responsibilities for the National Recreation Centre at Lilleshall.

Shortly before "kick off" an emissary from the opposition offered a paltry deal which Geof rejected.

Jim's evidence, delivered in an old world "educated " voice was short and effective: Geof was a reliable coach, capable of establishing excellent relations with outside bodies. On the question of dress he said that, on one or two occasions, Geoff's attire was what he would term "fashionably scruffy". He evoked an image of something a shade too casual for a Royal Garden Party.

It then fell to the BJA Chairman to make out the case for dismissal. Armed with a suit case full of files he attempted to give the impression that, more in sorrow than in anger, he had been driven reluctantly to deal with a turbulent priest. There was talk of sleepless nights, distress at the alienation of the press, Geof's slovenly clothing and failure of the Coaching Scheme to produce players of quality. It sounded persuasive until cross examination began.

The three members sitting in judgment were clearly bewildered by the summary dismissal, without prior warning, of a senior official who had not fiddled the funds or raped the secretary. On the contrary, he'd just been given an outstanding award for his services. So what were his unspeakable crimes?

Failure to wear a tie at the Crystal Palace? As they compared photographs of the National Coach and the Chairman, both without ties on that occasion, they must have wondered whether they were dealing with a sport or an escort agency! Antagonising the press? Geof's scrupulous corrections of false and absurd accusations seemed more worthy of praise than instant dismissal.

The most relevant charge was that Geof's coaching scheme had failed to produce top competitors. This was destroyed under cross examination. Peter Barnett, the Midland Area Coach, supplied our barrister with a large enough list of outstanding success by competitors trained in the Gleeson school to demolish this prejudiced assertion; and there was no mistaking the Tribunal's astonishment when the beleaguered Chairman asserted that employees are meant to be trodden on. Would the BJA reintroduce the stocks for typographical errors? "The Case for the Prosecution" was a disaster.

Our advocate concluded his masterly cross examination with a challenge: Since the case against Mr Gleeson was based on personal dislike amongst some influential London clubs, would it not be sensible to appoint a second National Coach to deal with them, and leave Mr Gleeson to serve the rest of the country where he was highly valued?

The Chairman saw the trap, and hesitated: "It was not for him to decide. It was for the Extraordinary General Meeting."

The Chairman of the Tribunal immediately ruled that we postpone the hearing until after the EGM We had crossed the Rubicon.

After checking with my London mole, I phoned Margaret Johnson at Grimsby:

"We're short of a few critical votes – and now they really are critical! The West are sending a coach full. Can your area find six more players to represent supportive Scottish clubs who can't afford the fares?"

"We'll do all we can to beat the buggers," said Margaret; and the day before the EGM a written quotation arrived from her which commenced; "At a time like this, God give us men . . ."

The Extraordinary General Meeting was held in a London hotel which was in no way extraordinary. Everything else was. An outsider might have suspected a carnival as over two hundred excited delegates flooded in. This was about five times the attendance at an Annual General Meeting.

Had I not been consumed with anger at the depths to which our Association had descended, I might have responded to the mood of an Alice in Wonderland trial and greeted some of the participants accordingly:

"Good afternoon, your Majesty. It is the King of Hearts, I presume. Having trouble with your lady wife? We don't want an outburst of impetuous tyranny, do we? Oh, I do apologise. I should have recognised you – a member of the Sports Council come to see fair play. Appearances are so deceptive. Then that isn't the Queen of Hearts? You do surprise me. I thought Humpty Dumpty was in the other book . . ."

"Who are all these bewildered gardeners you're wheeling in, Martin? Come for the trial? Verdicts at the ready, I hope. Don't be deterred by the evidence."

"And you, dear lady, must be the Duchess. No, I won't have a cigar, thank you; but do enjoy your own."

"Hello! Hello! It's good to see an old White Knight here. I remember you from your fighting days. No, you're quite right; GK would never have stood for this nonsense. Members of the Budokwai were gentlemen in those days."

But the irony would have been wasted. "Hicks has flipped his lid," they'd have said. "Thinks we're all part of a furry tile." Instead I acknowledged some sorrowful greetings with a rueful nod and sat down glumly at the side of the front row.

When all were assembled in their rival huddles a fish footman from the Executive bade us be seated; and the dignitaries mounted the rostrum. Tantantara zing boom!

At the first pretext I rose with my back to the dignitaries and informed the meeting of the disgraceful events at the Inquiry. I'm told I spoke with some vehemence and at times verged on a parody of Humpty Dumpty who made faces behind my back. It was not quite Alice's denunciation. That was yet to come.

However I succeeded in disrupting the Executive's contrived presentation; and this opened the floodgates to an astonishing series of impromptu declarations. An international competitor rose like the Mad Hatter summoned in the act of eating bread and jam to give his irrelevant evidence about murdering Time. He declared he had once had a reputable profession before his fall from grace. The audience were riveted by what promised to be a scandalous exposure; but he sat down without further revelations.

Danny da Costa did all that could be expected of a March Hare to lighten the mood. He regaled us with a surrealist account of a recent dream in which the Chairman turned Geof (or was it Danny?) into a toadstool. The Chairman's tolerant smile suggested he would welcome such an option. This was followed by a Mock Turtle who said that very morning he had met Mr Leggett, the old Turtle who taught us; but he was unable to articulate the wisdom the Tortoise had imparted. He only knew he taught us.

Finally Geof, the Knave of Hearts, was allowed to speak in his own defence; and quite suddenly we knew it wasn't a pantomime after all. Despite charges which were as laughable as stealing tarts, he managed a restrained and dignified explanation of the problems and conflicts facing any National Coach and him in particular. One was left wondering what all the fuss had been about, and whether it was now time to compete with the rush hour traffic.

But no trial is complete without a verdict. We needed a terminal vote. Why else the voting cards?

So the King and I scrutinised the counting of two separate votes. One endorsed the Executive's right to hire and fire, and the other required Geof to be reinstated; but it was, as my intelligence had predicted, "a damn close run thing".

This should have been the end of the whole wretched business, but a subsequent Executive Meeting overruled the vote for reinstatement. However, since the Chairman had virtually committed the Association to abide by the vote of the EGM the BJA were obliged to pay extravagant compensation in an out of court settlement.

Geof was able to finance retraining. He became the professional secretary of the British Association of National Coaches and author of some outstanding books. The BJA could not bring themselves to appoint another full time National Coach; until, after sixteen years of declining membership and further expensive litigation, new Chairmen began to rebuild.

However, Geof's "wind of change" blew away the mystique of the aspiring Shoguns, and released into the atmosphere irrepressible curiosity. Provincial judo survived independently, and dominated British squads. Unorthodox skills devised in Geof's Coaching "hothouse" were increasingly exploited by Britain's new World Champions. Above all, one no longer hears a beginner's earnest question rejected by an expert with the traditional evasion:

"Don't ask until you're a black belt; and then you won't need to ask."

Although the vote in Gleeson's favour was the conclusion of The Trial, it was not, for me, the climax. This came when Ivan Silver sprang up, smouldering with a fury which was only just under control, and delivered a devastating tirade against small minded bigotry that had pilloried an inspired pioneer.

"You're not worth all he's done for you," he yelled in crescendo. "I'm wasting my time here. I'd be better off at home watching 'The Planet of the Apes'. But why bother? You are 'The Planet of the Apes'." Then striding through the audience, which opened up as the Red Sea opened for Moses, he stormed out.

At this point the Queen should have screamed, "Off with his head! All creatures over a mile high must lose their heads."

And all the creatures in the courtroom should have risen up in protest at anyone having the temerity to challenge the Divine Right of Kings, Shoguns or any other Establishment. Soaring into the air in a maelstrom of anger and confusion, they would have fluttered down to be revealed as nothing but a pack of cards, fragments of ancient Japanese prints or the dead leaves of Autumn.

And then I should have awakened to find Danny da Costa telling me it was all a bad dream. It would have made a lovely ending.

But true stories often lack tidy endings – which is not necessarily a matter for regret. The passing of nearly twenty years has healed the most grievous wounds; and a new generation, which includes my own young family of judo players, will ensure that the story of our sport runs and runs. For, whatever judo was, it has become a sport, as our founder intended – a school sport – a Sports Council Sport – an International Sport – an Olympic Sport.

Some may pine nostalgically for the mystique of the old Shoguns, the "coveted black belt" and the deadly kiai. They may justifiably regret the materialism which now pervades professional sport. But "The Golden Age" is usually in the retrospective eye of the beholder. We recall most vividly the things we most enjoyed. I do. So why pine? Enjoy the rose tinted memories. I still have my beaver hat and the little green book by E.J.Harrison which introduced me to "the gentle art". They remind me of a lot of sweat, of twisted toes and sore armpits, of the curious beginnings of lifelong friendships and, most vividly, of some hilarious laughs.

Epilogue

"I have answered three questions, and that is enough,"
Said his father: "don't give yourself airs!
Do you think I can listen all day to such stuff?
Be off or I'll kick you down stairs!"

1974 seems an appropriate point to pause. Hamburg, Western Area success (and Danny's in particular), my last year as Area Coach and the "Gleeson Trial" all marked the end of an era.

However this was not the end of my judo activities – which is just as well, since I've retained my extravagant judo appetite. "Eat like a camel." advised Trevor Leggett. "You never know when you will eat again." So before the introduction of weight categories we always tried to avoid eating on an empty stomach. And old habits can be very comforting. The battle of the bulge is now being lost by attrition.

After '74 I ran one of Britain's first Centres of Excellence in Judokwai Bristol where my son, Simon, found his wife – Margaret; and where my daughter, Kim, met her husband – Bob Willingham. They all wear black belts and make an outstanding contribution to British judo as competitors, coaches, film makers and photographer.

George Kerr, the international competitor and coach, has twice been elected BJA Chairman; and, after the BJA's seventeen years of strategic coaching deprivation Seth Birch has been appointed as a full time National Coach. Both are breathing new life into British Judo – though not without some déjà vu resistance from aspiring Shoguns! Camaraderie is being rekindled. I'm sure GK would have been pleased.

Dave Clarke and Nick Strang have gallantly relieved me of the chairmanship and coaching responsibilities for Judokwai Bristol. I introduced Nick to judo over thirty years ago, and we've maintained a close friendship. He has a wealth of international experience and coaches with distinction. Unfortunately decline in school sport has had an adverse effect on youthful recruitment in all sports, and judo has been no exception. However, I have been in touch with No. 10 Downing Street on this matter, and been invited to the erstwhile home of our far sighted benefactor, Harold McMillan. I owe his successor some assistance.

Despite these peripheral difficulties, Judokwai Bristol continued for thirty years as the only judo establishment with a Baroque fountain –

albeit recently deprived of water; the national recession knows no frontiers. Indeed financial pressures have finally driven us out of Bristol University's Victoria Rooms. Never fear! Thanks to Dave's perch on the ladder, the phoenix is to rise yet again – this time from a Fire Station where there is an adequate water supply. I, therefore, hope to don judo-gi once a week for a little longer, and secure it with the red and white belt of a 6th. Dan with which I have been honoured.

Geof Gleeson died unexpectedly in February of this year. The BJA was roused by George Kerr to award him a posthumous 9th Dan – the highest grade ever achieved in Great Britain. His funeral service was a wonderful celebration of a creative and inspiring life. It was crowded with friends and colleagues who stirred many memories of halcyon days at Lilleshall and Karlshrue when we seemed to be in the vanguard of life itself. I was privileged to be amongst those whom Diki Gleeson invited to speak about her husband's life. She didn't want the addresses to exclude all humour.

Geof's last present to my family was some Japanese stepping stones. He explained that they should be laid in an irregular line, so that one cannot walk over them without looking down and enjoying their design; and when looking up after each change of direction a new vista is revealed. He relished every foothold of his life; and those who, for a while, trod the same stones shared his vision and remain a little starry eyed.

My godson Finn Gleeson, who trained at Judokwai Bristol, has been awarded his black belt in Japan. Geof, who was engaged on the definitive biography of Professor Kano, visited his son in Tokyo. It was his first return after forty years. He astonished Nick on a subsequent visit to Bristol by commenting that Judokwai Bristol now has a stronger membership than the Kodokan! It is sad to reflect that the Japanese club recommended by Harrison as the "fountain head" of judo once had more black belts on their tatami than in all the clubs in Britain combined. For better or worse, the days of Japanese domination have passed.

A few years ago, when the Gleesons and ourselves were staying with the Da Costa family in Torquay, Danny said quite spontaneously:

"Let's pay Jim Vicars a surprise visit at Chagford and have a barbecue in his garden. And let's invite Ivan Silver. We haven't seen him for years, and it might be his birthday."

Jim is a splendid, swashbuckling ex-Bristol black belt, originally from Scotland. When he arrived home astride a magnificent horse, the smell of burnt sausages led him to a crowd of old friends merrily ensconced on the lawn of his rural retreat. The warmth of his welcome was not diminished by even a quiver of surprise. And Ivan travelled over a hundred miles to join us – even though it wasn't his birthday. There's more to judo than fighting.

November 1994.

BIBLIOGRAPHY

Alice in Wonderland   Lewis Carroll
Alice Through the Looking Glass   Lewis Carroll
Scouting for Boys   Baden Powell
The Complete Sherlock Holmes   Sir Arthur Conan Doyle
The Art of Ju-Jitsu   E.J. Harrison
Brazillian Adventure   Peter Fleming
Beau Geste   P.C. Wren
My Study of Judo   Gunji Koizumi
Judo for the West   Geof Gleeson
All About Judo   Geof Gleeson
The Mikado   Gilbert and Sullivan
Iolanthe   Gilbert and Sullivan
The Way to the Top   foreword by HRH The Duke of Edinburgh